Beyond Circle

I0408980

India to Germany
"Immigration and Job Searching Guide"

2023 Edition

This book is a tribute to the brave souls who envision a brighter future beyond the familiar shores of their homeland. It is a guide for those who seek to expand their horizons, explore new cultures, and embrace the challenges that come with international migration. Specifically, it serves as a roadmap for those who aspire to live a life filled with growth, fulfilment, and success in Germany.

May the pages of this book be a source of hope and knowledge, guiding you as you embark on this life-changing journey. Remember that dedication is the fuel that propels dreams into reality. Your resilience, unwavering commitment, and passion will shape your destiny.

Although the path to a new life may be uncertain, with dedication, you can conquer any uncertainty and forge a future of promise and possibility. Through the highs and lows, the triumphs and setbacks, stay steadfast in your pursuit. This book is a tribute to your courage, determination, and unyielding spirit.

As you read through these pages, remember that you are not alone in your journey. Countless others have tread similar paths before you, and their successes serve as an inspiration. So, with determination in your heart and this guide in your hands, set forth on your voyage from India to Germany, ready to embrace every opportunity that comes your way. Here's to the dreamers, the seekers, and the believers—may your dedication light the way to a world of endless possibilities.

CONTENTS

Introduction

Welcome to "India to Germany: Immigration and Job Searching Guide." This comprehensive book is designed to be your reliable companion on the path to success as you embark on the life-changing journey of moving from India to Germany. Whether you're pursuing new career opportunities or seeking to enhance your educational prospects, this guide will serve as an invaluable resource to make your dream a reality.

Embarking on a new journey can be daunting, but fear not! The book "India to Germany" is your trusty guide, providing crucial information and practical advice to ensure a smooth transition to your new life in Germany. Each chapter covers essential aspects of the immigration process, equipping you with the knowledge you need to navigate this exciting new chapter in your life successfully.

Germany offers a multitude of advantages for those who choose to immigrate. With a strong economy, excellent healthcare and education systems, and a welcoming society, Germany truly has something for everyone. By understanding the benefits of immigrating, you can confidently take the necessary steps to make your dream of living in Germany a reality.

At the heart of any successful immigration journey is language proficiency. By mastering German, you not only improve your daily life but also increase your chances of success in the job market and in integrating into German society. We will guide you through the requirements, certifications, and language course options to help you achieve your language goals.

Choosing the right immigration category is crucial for a

smooth transition. Our comprehensive guide will help you navigate the various options and determine the best route for your unique circumstances, whether it be through a job offer or educational pursuit.

Although the application process may seem daunting, we have broken down the steps to make it easier for you to gather the necessary documents and navigate the bureaucracy.

In today's ever-changing job market, it's important to stay ahead of the game. Our guide provides expert tips and a well-crafted job-hunting plan to help you successfully navigate this evolving landscape. From crafting an impressive resume to effectively utilizing LinkedIn, we will equip you with the knowledge needed to stand out from the competition.

As you progress to the interview stage, we have prepared a "Power Pack Interview Mantra" to help you excel in both online and in-person interviews. Our tips and insights will give you the edge needed to impress potential employers and secure your dream job.

Understanding the financial aspects of your move is also important. In the "Money Matters" chapter, we will delve into compensation packages, pay structures, and salary negotiation strategies to ensure that you receive a fair and competitive offer.

Our "India to Germany: Immigration and Job Searching Guide" is designed to empower you with the knowledge and skills necessary to make your move to Germany a success. Remember that your journey is about embracing new opportunities, overcoming challenges, and creating lasting memories. We wish you the best of luck on this transformative adventure to Germany!

Chapter One

INTRODUCTION TO GERMANY

Germany, officially known as the Federal Republic of Germany, is a country situated in Central Europe. It shares borders with several countries, including Denmark, Poland, the Czech Republic, Austria, Switzerland, France, Luxembourg, Belgium, and the Netherlands. Germany is a prominent player on the global stage thanks to its rich history, vibrant culture, and robust economy.

Germany has a complex history that covers the Holy Roman Empire, the Protestant Reformation, the Age of Enlightenment, the Napoleonic Wars, the unification of Germany in 1871, and the turbulent events of the 20th century, including World War I, the rise of Nazism, and World War II.

After World War II, East Germany (German Democratic Republic) and West Germany (Federal Republic of Germany) emerged. The country was reunified in 1989 after the fall of the Berlin Wall.

German culture is diverse and influenced by regional differences. It contributes to music, literature, philosophy, art, and science. Germany has produced famous composers like Bach, Beethoven, and Wagner and renowned philosophers like Kant and Nietzsche. German festivals like Oktoberfest in Munich showcase the country's rich folk traditions, music, dance, and cuisine.

The official language of Germany is German, spoken by most of the population. Germany has significantly contributed to world literature, with numerous acclaimed German-language authors and poets.

Germany boasts several vibrant and historic cities. Berlin, the capital and largest city is known for its cosmopolitan atmosphere, world-class museums, and iconic landmarks like the Brandenburg Gate and Berlin Wall. Munich is famous for its Oktoberfest celebration, while Hamburg is known for its bustling port and maritime heritage. Other notable cities include Frankfurt, Cologne, Stuttgart, and Leipzig. Germany is also home to picturesque landscapes like the Black Forest, the Rhine Valley, the Bavarian Alps, and enchanting castles, including Neuschwanstein Castle.

Germany has one of the largest and most potent economies globally. It is known for its strong manufacturing sector, particularly in the automotive industry, and its contributions to technology, engineering, pharmaceuticals, and renewable energy. Germany is the largest European Union economy and a significant exporter of goods.

It also has a robust education system and is renowned for its universities and research institutions. It has produced numerous Nobel laureates and is recognized as a scientific research and innovation hub. The country has high rankings in quality-of-life indicators such as healthcare, education, safety, and social welfare. It boasts a well-established infrastructure, reliable public transportation systems, and a superior standard of living.

German cuisine is diverse and varies across different regions. Traditional dishes include bratwurst (sausage), sauerkraut (fermented cabbage), pretzels, schnitzel (breaded and fried meat cutlets), and various types of bread, pastries, and cakes. Germany is also known for its beer, with multiple styles and breweries.

In short, Germany's rich history, strong economy, cultural contributions, and high quality of life make it a desirable destination for visitors, students, and professionals worldwide. Whether you want to explore its historical sites, immerse yourself in its culture, or experience its technological advancements, Germany offers a unique and diverse experience for those who visit or call it home.

Advantages of Immigration to Germany

If you plan to relocate to Germany, there are numerous compelling reasons to do so. Here are some crucial factors that you should consider.

Germany has a strong economy and offers many job opportunities in various industries, such as automotive manufacturing, engineering, technology, pharmaceuticals, finance, and renewable energy. The country's high wages and low unemployment rate make it an attractive destination for professionals seeking career growth and economic stability.

Germany is renowned for its excellent quality of life. The country's robust healthcare system, dependable infrastructure, efficient public transportation, quality education, and reliable social welfare system all attest to its excellence. The German people prioritize work-life balance, environmental sustainability, and social inclusivity, all of which contribute to an exceptional standard of living for residents. Germany is renowned for its outstanding universities and research institutions that offer a range of academic programs, including undergraduate and postgraduate degrees, vocational training, and specialized research opportunities. The country's dedication to education, innovation, and research makes it an ideal destination for students and professionals looking to expand their knowledge and advance their careers.

Germany is home to a rich and diverse cultural heritage featuring an array of historical landmarks, museums, art galleries, and cultural festivities. The country has an impressive influence on music, literature, philosophy, and the arts. Visitors can explore the historic streets of Berlin, admire magnificent castles, and enjoy traditional Oktoberfest celebrations, all within a vibrant cultural atmosphere that attracts people worldwide.

Thanks to its central location in Europe, Germany is an excellent starting point for exploring the rest of the continent. With well-connected transportation networks, including extensive rail and air travel options, visitors can easily travel to nearby countries and experience different cultures, landscapes, and attractions. Living in Germany also offers the convenience of exploring Europe's beauty.

Germany is an inclusive and diverse society that welcomes people from all backgrounds. The country has established integration programs and initiatives to help immigrants settle and transition, including language courses, cultural orientation, and employment assistance. This fact makes it easier for immigrants to become part of German society.

Germany is recognized for its forward-thinking policies, dedication to addressing social concerns, and emphasis on inclusivity and social justice. The country is leading in combating climate change and places significant importance on sustainability, renewable energy, gender equality, and LGBTQ+ rights. These values make Germany an attractive destination for those who prioritize these traits.

Germany is also renowned for its exceptional safety and security standards. The country boasts a robust legal system, efficient law enforcement agencies, and a meagre crime rate. Residents enjoy a peaceful living environment and a sense of personal safety.

How to immigrate?

If you're an Indian planning to immigrate to Germany in 2023, you need to follow specific procedures and requirements. To help you get started, we've outlined the general steps involved. We recommend researching the different immigration options available to you and carefully reviewing their requirements, eligibility criteria, and application processes. Some popular pathways include skilled worker programs, study programs, and family reunification.

Suppose you are an Indian interested in immigrating to Germany. In that case, it's essential to research and understand the various immigration options available. Some possible pathways include:

Germany offers skilled worker programs for IT, engineering, healthcare, and academia professionals. Researching the specific qualifications, work experience requirements, and job market conditions for each program is essential. You can also explore research universities and courses that align with your interests and academic qualifications. Learn about the admission requirements, tuition fees, available scholarships, and potential job opportunities after graduation.

Do you have family members living legally in Germany? If so, they might be able to help you immigrate through family reunification. However, it's essential to understand the eligibility criteria and document requirements beforehand. Immigration requirements and qualifications vary depending on the category, including age, education, work experience, language skills, health insurance, and financial stability. It's crucial to pay attention to the specific criteria for the immigration path you have chosen. If you intend to immigrate to Germany, you may need to have proficiency in the German language. The required ability level varies depending on the immigration category, and you may need to take language courses or programs to meet the necessary language requirements. Additionally, recognized language tests such as TestDaF or Goethe-Zertifikat may be required for certification.

For reliable and current information on immigration regulations, procedures and prerequisites, it's best to consult official sources such as the German embassy or consulate in

India, the Federal Office for Migration and Refugees (BAMF), or the German government's official immigration portal.

To increase your chances, it's essential to research and understand the different options available to you. It will help you prepare for the requirements and choose the best pathway.

If you plan on immigrating to Germany, having a good command of the German language is essential as most immigration categories require German language proficiency. To improve your language skills, consider enrolling in language courses and obtaining a recognized language certification like the TestDaF or Goethe-Zertifikat.

When determining the appropriate immigration category for your situation and objectives, there are several options to choose from, including the Job Seeker Visa, EU Blue Card, Student Visa, or Family Reunification Visa. If you intend to work in Germany, having a job offer from a German employer would be advantageous. Alternatively, if you're interested in furthering your education, seek admission to a recognized German university or educational institution.

To successfully apply for your immigration category, make sure you have all the necessary documents, including educational certificates, language test results, work experience documents, financial statements, and a valid passport. You must submit your application to the embassy, consulate, or immigration office in India, and carefully follow the instructions, pay the necessary fees, and include all the required documents.

To be granted a residence permit, you must have health insurance coverage that meets the requirements set by Germany. Make sure you obtain the necessary coverage.

The processing time for immigration applications is not fixed and can vary. It's essential to remain patient and wait for a decision on your application. You may also be required to undergo interviews or provide more information during this stage.

Once your application is approved, you will be granted a residence permit. Make all necessary travel arrangements and plan your arrival in Germany accordingly. It is vital to comply with any quarantine or COVID-19-related regulations that may be in place at the time of your arrival.

Upon arrival in Germany, register your address at the local registration office (Einwohnermeldeamt) within the specified time frame. Familiarize yourself with the local rules and culture, and start settling into your new life.

It's important to note that immigration policies and procedures can change over time, so it's advisable to consult the official websites of the German embassy or consulate in India for the most up-to-date and accurate information. Additionally, seeking assistance from an immigration lawyer or a reputable immigration consultancy can help ensure a smoother process.

Importance of German Language

If you're planning to immigrate to Germany, it's important to have German language proficiency. Here are some important details to keep in mind:

a. Language Requirement:

To be eligible for immigration to Germany, it is generally necessary to have proficiency in the German language, as it is a German-speaking country. However, the level of language proficiency required can vary depending on the specific immigration pathway you choose.

b. Language Certifications:

You may need to obtain a recognized language certification to prove your German language skills. Standard certifications accepted in Germany include the TestDaF (Test Deutsch als Fremdsprache) and the Goethe-Zertifikat. These exams assess your listening, reading, writing, and speaking abilities in German.

c. Language Courses:

Consider enrolling in language courses if you want to enhance your German language skills. You can search for language schools or institutions that offer courses tailored for immigrants or individuals who plan to study or work in Germany. These courses will assist you in attaining the necessary level of language proficiency.

d. Self-Study:

If you are unable to attend formal language courses, there are alternative options available for learning German such as self-study using textbooks, online resources, language learning apps, and language exchange programs. It is essential to set aside regular practice time and fully immerse yourself in the language.

e. Language Exemptions:

In some cases, specific immigration categories or programs may offer exemptions or relaxed language requirements. For example, English-taught degree programs at German universities may require something other than German language skills. However, learning some German to ease your daily life in Germany is still beneficial.

f. Integration Courses:

When you get to Germany, the government may provide you with integration courses (Integrationskurse) in which you can participate. These courses will give you German language lessons and cultural orientation to help you adjust to life in Germany.

g. Continuous Learning:

Learning German is not only essential for the immigration process but also for your long-term success and integration in

Germany. Even if you meet the minimum language requirements for immigration, continuous learning and improving your German language skills will benefit you professionally and socially.

It's essential to remember that having good language skills is crucial when applying for immigration. Investing time and energy into improving your German language proficiency can boost your chances of success and enhance your possibilities for employment, education, and integration in Germany.

Choose an Immigration Category

When looking to immigrate to Germany, choosing the right pathway or visa category that fits your situation and goals is significant. Here are some factors to keep in mind:

Germany offers various pathways for skilled workers, students, job seekers, families seeking reunification, entrepreneurs, and others. The EU Blue Card is the most common program for skilled workers, allowing highly skilled professionals to live and work in Germany. To obtain a Blue Card, you must have a degree from a recognized university, a job offer that meets a minimum salary requirement, and proficiency in the German language (if required).

You can apply for a student visa if you plan to pursue higher education in Germany. Research universities and programs that align with your academic interests and qualifications, and check the admission requirements, tuition fees, scholarships and any additional prerequisites for international students.

The Job Seeker Visa allows individuals to stay in Germany for a limited period while searching for employment opportunities. Suppose you have immediate family members who are legal residents or citizens of Germany. In that case, you may be eligible for family reunification, which allows spouses, children, and dependent family members to join their relatives in Germany.

For individuals who want to start a business or invest in a German company, Germany offers an Entrepreneur Visa. This category requires a solid business plan, proof of funds, and potential job creation or economic benefit for Germany.

Apart from these categories, there may be other immigration options depending on your specific circumstances. When choosing an immigration category, consider your qualifications, work experience, language proficiency, financial situation, and long-term goals. Each immigration category has its requirements and documentation, so it is vital to thoroughly research the specific requirements for your chosen type and ensure that you meet all the criteria before proceeding with the application process.

Consulting official resources such as the website of the German embassy or consulate in your country, or seeking advice from immigration lawyers or reputable immigration consultancies, can provide valuable guidance in selecting the most appropriate immigration category for your circumstances.

Job Offer or Education

Suppose you are planning to immigrate to Germany for work. In that case, obtaining a job offer from a German employer is advantageous as it shows that you have secured employment and can contribute to the German economy. You can research job opportunities, network with professionals, and utilize online job portals or recruitment agencies specializing in international placements to achieve this.

To enhance your chances of success, you should familiarize yourself with the German job market and understand the demand for your skills and qualifications through job market research. You can also network with professionals in your field through social media platforms like LinkedIn, attend industry events, and engage in online forums or communities.

Suppose your goal is to pursue higher education in Germany. In that case, you should research universities and programs that align with your academic interests and qualifications. You should also follow the application procedures for job applications or education admissions and tailor your application materials, such as your resume/CV and cover letter, to showcase your skills and qualifications in a way that aligns with German standards.

Depending on the job or education program, you may need to meet specific language requirements. Most job offers typically require German language proficiency, although some multinational companies may conduct business in English. Education programs may also have language requirements for the language of instruction or integration purposes.

Germany offers work opportunities for international students during their studies and after graduation. It would be best to familiarize yourself with the regulations and conditions for working alongside your studies or seeking employment after completing your degree. Additionally, internships or traineeships can be a valuable way to gain work experience in Germany, potentially leading to job offers.

Being proactive, persistent, and patient during the job search or application process is essential. Remember that securing a job offer or admission to an educational institution demonstrates your commitment and readiness to contribute to German society. You can seek guidance from career services or professionals in your field if needed.

Required Documents

To ensure that your immigration application to Germany goes smoothly, create a document checklist that meets the specific requirements of your chosen category. Review the official guidelines provided by the German embassy or consulate in your country or the relevant immigration authority's website to avoid omissions or delays.

Ensure your passport is valid for the duration of your stay in Germany and meets the specific validity requirements of your immigration category. If your passport is nearing expiration, consider renewing it before submitting your application.

Gather your educational certificates, diplomas, degrees, or transcripts, ensuring they are duly attested or certified, depending on the requirements. You may need to provide certified translations if they are not in German or English.

If your immigration category requires work experience, gather relevant documents like employment letters, contracts, or any other evidence of your professional experience, highlighting your job responsibilities, employment duration, and roles.

If you have obtained language certifications, include them in your application package to demonstrate your proficiency in the German language, which is often a requirement for immigration.

Depending on your immigration category, you may need proof of financial stability, such as bank statements, proof of income, or sponsorship letters. Obtain health insurance that meets the specific requirements of your immigration category, as Germany requires residents to have health insurance coverage.

Complete the application forms specific to your immigration category, ensuring they are accurately filled out and include any required signatures or additional information.

Depending on your circumstances and the specific requirements of your chosen immigration category, you may need to provide additional documents like a motivation letter, proof of accommodation in Germany, marriage or birth certificates, or any other relevant documentation.

Prepare both original documents and copies as required, following the instructions provided by the immigration authorities regarding which documents need to be submitted in original form and which ones can be copies.

It's essential to carefully review the document requirements and gather all the necessary documents to support your application, as complete documentation can lead to delays or rejection of your application. If you have any doubts or concerns, refer to the official guidelines or seek assistance from an immigration lawyer or consultancy to ensure your application package is complete and accurate.

Application Process

To submit your immigration application to the German embassy, consulate, or immigration office in India, you need to follow some important details. Firstly, fill out the necessary application forms with accurate and complete information. Check for any required signatures or additional documents.

Next, organize your documents per the guidelines provided by the German embassy or consulate, ensuring that all necessary documents are included, and copies of originals are made. Follow the order specified to speed up the application review process.

Check the application fees and payment methods required for your immigration category, and make sure to prepare the necessary funds in the accepted currency and form. Different submission methods may apply to various embassies or consulates, so confirm the submission method and any specific requirements through the official website or by contacting the respective German embassy or consulate.

Be mindful of the application deadlines specified for your immigration category, and submit your application well in advance to allow for processing time and potential delays.

Depending on the immigration category, you may be required to attend an interview or provide biometric data (such as fingerprints and photographs), so follow the instructions provided by the embassy or consulate regarding these additional requirements.

Maintain a record of your application details, including any reference numbers or tracking information provided by the embassy or consulate, to track the progress of your application and communicate with the relevant authorities if needed.

During the application process, you may receive requests for additional information or documentation from the immigration authorities. Respond to these requests promptly and within the specified timeframe.

Upon submission of your application, you may receive a confirmation or receipt, which serves as proof that your application has been submitted. Keep this document safe.

The processing time for immigration applications can vary depending on factors such as the immigration category and workload of the immigration authorities. Be patient and allow sufficient time for the processing of your application. Follow the instructions carefully to avoid delays or rejection of your application. Seek assistance from an immigration lawyer or consultancy if you have any doubts or concerns.

Application Processing Time

The processing time for immigration applications can vary based on various factors, including immigration category, the workload of immigration authorities, and external factors. While official processing times from the German embassy or consulate can provide an estimate, actual processing times may differ.

It's advisable only to make frequent inquiries about your

application's status if it has exceeded the expected processing time. Constant questions may disrupt the workflow and delay the process. However, if you have specific concerns or your application has exceeded the indicated processing time, you can contact the embassy or consulate for an update.

The embassy, consulate, or immigration authorities will notify you of a decision on your application, either an approval, rejection or request for additional information or documents. If the authorities need more information or documentation, respond promptly within the specified timeframe to avoid rejection.

Ensure that the contact information in your application remains accurate and up-to-date, including email, phone, and mailing address. If any changes occur, inform the immigration authorities immediately to ensure you receive important notifications or requests.

While waiting to process your application, use this time to prepare for the next steps in your immigration journey. Keep copies of all documents submitted with your application and any correspondence or notifications received from the embassy or consulate.

Immigration processes can be complex, and delays are not uncommon. It's important to remain patient and flexible throughout the waiting period. Stay informed about any updates or changes in immigration policies or procedures that may affect your application.

Remember that processing times and procedures can vary depending on your immigration category and circumstances. Follow the instructions the embassy or consulate provides and respond promptly to any requests for additional information or documents. Contact the embassy or consulate directly if you have concerns or questions about your application's processing.

Interview or Medical Examination

As part of your application process for immigration to Germany, you may be required to attend an interview based on your specific immigration category and individual circumstances. The interview aims to evaluate your eligibility, intentions, and suitability for immigration.

To prepare for the interview, familiarize yourself with the requirements and expectations outlined by the German embassy or consulate. Research common interview questions related to your immigration category and prepare thoughtful and honest responses. Practice your answers to ensure clarity and confidence during the interview.

Ensure you bring all the necessary documents and identification, including your passport, application forms, supporting documents, and any other requested documents. It's essential to have both original documents and copies as required.

Dress appropriately for the interview, presenting yourself professionally and respectfully. Follow any guidelines or cultural norms regarding attire specified by the embassy or consulate.

Depending on your immigration category, the interview may be conducted in German or English. Ensure that you are prepared to communicate effectively in the designated language. Practice your language skills to ensure clarity and comprehension during the interview.

Some immigration categories require medical examinations to assess an applicant's health and fitness for immigration. The embassy or consulate will provide a list of approved panel physicians or medical facilities where you can undergo the required medical examinations. Ensure that you visit an approved physician or facility to ensure the validity and acceptance of the medical report.

Contact the approved panel physicians or medical facilities to schedule your appointment for the medical examination. Follow their instructions regarding preparation, required documents, and specific procedures or tests. After the medical examination, you will receive a medical report detailing your health status. Please keep a copy of the medical report for your records and submit it as instructed by the German embassy or consulate.

It's crucial to follow the instructions provided by the embassy or consulate regarding interviews and medical examinations. Attend all appointments as scheduled, arrive on time, and follow any additional guidelines or requirements. Remember to be honest, cooperative, and respectful during interviews and medical examinations. Provide accurate information and respond truthfully to any questions asked. Contact the German embassy or consulate for guidance and clarification if you have any concerns or questions regarding interviews or medical examinations.

Receive Decision on Your Application

After you have submitted your application to the German embassy, consulate, or immigration authorities, they will inform you of their decision. The decision may be an approval, rejection, or a request for additional information or documents.

If your application is approved, you will receive an approval notice or visa permitting you to immigrate to Germany. However, the approval notice may also specify any restrictions on your immigration status, such as the duration of your stay or work limitations.

On the other hand, if your application is rejected, you will receive a notice explaining the reasons for the decision. You may have the option to appeal the decision or reapply, depending on the circumstances and immigration category.

Sometimes, the immigration authorities may request additional information or documents to complete the evaluation of your application. It is crucial to provide the requested information within the specified timeframe, or it may result in a rejection of your application.

If your application is approved, you must follow the procedures the German embassy or consulate outlines to obtain the physical visa sticker or permit in your passport. Make sure to understand the conditions and obligations associated with your immigration status.

Please keep copies of all the documents related to your application for future reference, as they may be required for appeals or follow-up procedures.

Once you receive a decision on your application, take timely action based on the outcome. If you have any questions or concerns, contact the German embassy or consulate, or seek professional advice to ensure that you are well informed and can take the necessary steps accordingly.

Relocation and Settlement

Congratulations on having your immigration application approved and receiving your visa to Germany! To ensure a smooth transition, making necessary arrangements before your travel is essential. This includes booking flights, arranging transportation to your destination, and considering any COVID-19-related travel requirements or restrictions.

Upon arrival, one of the first things to do is to secure accommodation in Germany. This can be done by renting an apartment, staying with friends or family, or booking temporary accommodation such as a hotel or serviced apartment. Research the housing options available in your chosen city or region and consider location, cost, and proximity to amenities.

Preparing a budget for your relocation and settlement in Germany is also essential. Consider expenses such as housing, utilities, transportation, groceries, healthcare, and other living costs. Ensure you have sufficient funds to cover your initial expenses until you secure employment or settle into your new situation.

Make arrangements for health insurance coverage in Germany. Determine whether you are eligible for the statutory health insurance system or if you need to obtain private health insurance. Familiarize yourself with the healthcare system in Germany and understand the coverage and services available.

If you need to improve in German, consider enrolling in language courses or programs to improve your language skills. Communicating effectively in German will significantly facilitate your settlement and integration into German society.

Familiarize yourself with German culture, customs, and

social norms. Research and learn about the local traditions, etiquette, and values. Understanding and respecting cultural differences will help you navigate your new environment and foster positive interactions with locals.

Connect with local communities, expatriate groups, or others who share your interests or background. Join social or professional networks, attend events or workshops, and participate in community activities. Building a support network and engaging with the local community will assist in your integration and provide a sense of belonging.

Explore job opportunities in Germany if you have yet to secure employment before arrival. Update your resume or curriculum vitae to align with German standards, and consider translating it into German. Use online job portals, professional networks, and local job fairs to find suitable positions. Networking and reaching out to potential employers or recruiters can also be beneficial.

Upon arrival, complete necessary administrative tasks such as registering your residence, obtaining a tax identification number, and setting up a bank account. Familiarize yourself with the administrative procedures and requirements specific to your location in Germany.

Seek out resources and support services that can assist you in settling into your new life in Germany. This may include orientation programs, cultural integration courses, or mentorship programs. Take advantage of these resources to navigate the initial challenges of relocation and make a smooth transition.

Remember to be open-minded, patient, and proactive in seeking assistance or information when needed. Relocation and settlement can be a gradual process, and it may take time to adjust to your new environment. Embrace the opportunities for personal and professional growth that your new life in Germany can offer.

Chapter Two

JOB SEARCHING IN GERMANY

Looking and applying for jobs in Germany is not as easy and straightforward as it used to be in the past. Gone are the days of physically submitting or mailing your resume and waiting for a phone call for a job interview.

Nowadays, almost all employment communications take place electronically. Since the employer is unlikely to see your face or interact with you until you have the opportunity to demonstrate your qualifications in an interview, digital transformation and globalization have completely changed the dynamics of the job market. This includes the reliance on applicant tracking systems, web portals, and third-party recruiters, which have become integral parts of the job search process.

We are currently living in an online world where the internet has significantly impacted the job search mechanism. When it's time to start a job search, it's worth considering the statistics and identifying what actually yields results. Referrals have shown to be an effective way to secure a job interview quickly, bypassing the bureaucracy that exists in the job search process.

Research indicates that referrals are the most practical and reliable way to secure your next job offer. It is recommended to start with your network of people who know you well, such as friends, family, former colleagues, managers, and customers. Inform them that you are job hunting and ask for their assistance and guidance, showing appreciation for any help they can provide. This should be your first choice.

Attending business conferences, alumni reunions, and training programs presents excellent opportunities to approach and interact with potential influencers. While this approach may be slower, it should still be part of your job-hunting strategy. Find relevant networking events and actively participate, making sure to contribute positively and catch the attention of individuals who could potentially hire you for your next job.

When actively job searching, the internet can be a valuable ally. Online job portals, career pages, and recruiters offer numerous chances to connect with prospective employers. Establishing a strong online presence is crucial in setting yourself apart from other candidates and building a professional digital footprint.

To effectively search and utilize the internet to your advantage, it is important to conduct a thorough and strategic search using relevant keywords. Your resume should be specific and tailored to the job requirements, increasing your chances of success. Analysing job descriptions and incorporating the language, terms, and prerequisites commonly used by employers into your resume is the simplest and most effective way to begin. The more accurately and genuinely you integrate the language of prospective employers into your resume, the higher the likelihood of securing job interviews.

While the internet can be a great partner in job searching, directly applying to job postings online is a viable method, depending on the type of work and industry. However, it's important to understand that it may not yield instant results. Patience is key. You may apply to 100 jobs but receive an interview call from only one. On the other hand, referrals and networking are the fastest ways to secure an interview and save a significant amount of time.

Does that mean you should abandon your online job search and stop applying? Not at all. Instead, you should adjust your approach. Focus on the required skills and competencies that align with your profile. Include relevant keywords based on the job description. When you come across an attractive job opening, reach out to your LinkedIn network or leverage connections through friends and family who may have contacts in the organization. If you find a relevant connection, ask them to forward your resume and advocate for you. The chances of a favorable outcome increase significantly compared to blindly submitting job applications online.

If you don't have a direct connection, you can still try to connect with hiring managers or recruiters in the organization. It is generally easy to communicate with them online or through phone calls to discuss your interest in the position. Not everyone you reach out to will be responsive or able to assist you. Nevertheless, it will help to move you from being seen as an "online candidate" to a "real interested candidate." This may look like a minor aspect, yet it is most certainly not. As the numbers appear, having a genuine live individual included can have a significant effect.

COVID-19 Reshaping Job Hunting

As you all know, 2020 began with COVID-19, which turned into a crisis quite swiftly. According to ILO, the effect of the COVID-19 pandemic on the labour market shows the devastating impact on workers and businesses. In a press release on 29 April 2020, ILO reported a sharp decline in global working hours.

More than 436 million businesses worldwide face a significant risk of disruption. These companies operate in the hit economies, with some 232 million in wholesale and retail firms, 111 million in manufacturing, 51 million in accommodation and food services and 42 million in property and other businesses.

According to some studies, the coronavirus pandemic could lead to the loss of 47 million jobs in USA. Many people have already lost their jobs, which resulted into significant increase in jobless claims.

According to Spiegel, coronavirus hit the German economy hard. German government received 470,000 requests for short working hours' incentives that prohibit layoffs for workers, 20 times more than the financial crisis in 2009.

I personally believe that Post-COVID-19 world will look different. The situation may swing in either direction; millions of workers losing their jobs worldwide may instigate strong and fierce competition. On the other hand, it is an opportunity for everyone to recalibrate his or her position. Employers may be laying off workers or reducing the working hours during the time of the pandemic. Nevertheless, once the crisis will subside, which will certainly, and then you should be ready to ramp up quickly.

If you are a fresh graduate and looking for your first big opportunity or you have lost your job during this crisis, take your time to redefine your job-hunting strategy, recalibrate your job hunting materials, update and refine your LinkedIn profile, focus on networking and learn new skills via online courses.

Consider all the available options, for example, switching to a different industry or function. Consider options to work remotely. However, do not quit searching for a career, now more than ever you need to get it up.

Just be in the game and do not leave the playing field. If you are not there, many others will be there to grab the opportunity.

Dynamics of "Job Search"

You also have to realise, how much career quest over the last decade has shifted. If you think about it, we used to get a job back in the day, we will work in a company all our lives, and these days are gone. Statistics indicate that in the next five years as many as half of the population will be self-contractors.

When you think about it, that's pretty mind blowing.

Every employment now is temporary, and in your lifetime, you will have to search out for work repeatedly. You are no longer an employee. You are a service provider. Consider yourself as business of one. Precisely, what does this mean?

Well, if you have to look for work, frequently, you will not work for that employer, you will work with your partner. You will offer them your services. That means you have to show your value constantly. Can you market yourselves? Do you know what value you can offer to an employer and how can it be explained? Here is the secret. This is what is required in today's job search so that you can continue to work and enjoy the best career opportunity.

This is an exciting time to think about what you can do for yourself and your career. Especially when you know precisely, and what you should say to people whom you want to impress and connect. If you can unload and understand and to embrace it as a business.

Think of this, then. Consider the future of your company. What do you want? How can it be sold? How can you show your value and deliver it to the very people you want to reach?

Employment is crucial to earn a livelihood and to live a respectable life. Majority of graduates join the labour force after completing their formal education, while some start their own businesses. Percentage of individuals seeking employment is increasing rapidly. All of us living in capitalist economies must work for wages; the inability to obtain a job means no income. You really have to be very competitive in your job hunt.

Every job opening receives hundreds of resumes on average, but only four to five of the candidates will receive an interview call, and only one of those will be offered a job. To grab your dream job is difficult but not impossible. You can get a job of your choice easily by following specific standards.

New technologies have an impact on the business world, so maybe new jobs have emerged? Either way, job hunters should get more information about the latest trends; to prepare for job searching.

Whether you are a fresh graduate or experienced professional, these are the apparent job search trends.

Trends Reshaping Recruitment

Many factors, including artificial intelligence, digital transformation and technological advancements, are changing the dynamics of recruiting constantly. Now COVID-19 crisis has significantly changed the job market.

High Demand for Soft Skills

According to a report published by Progressive Policy Institute USA in 2019, shows that nearly 7 million jobs were unfulfilled! By 2020, the number will most likely be much higher due to the increasing skill gap. What kind of skills do you lack? If you want to find a job, what skills should you develop? Study shows that soft skills throughout 2020 will be highly popular. This means that the soft skills in the resume shall increase your chances to win an interview.

Focus on Learning

Owing to the lack of skills, many companies give their employees new opportunities for learning. Over the previous year, businesses have increased their staff training budgets, and the trend is expected to remain steady. Firms concentrate primarily on building talent pipelines and searching for openings from within the company by supplying existing workers with training and skill development opportunities. They offer internships for young adults. Employees will move forward in their careers, and employees are more likely to remain longer with an organisation.

Remote Working

Remote work will help both staff and employers, and there is actually an increase in the number of remote jobs. More than 4.3 million people in the USA work at least half the time remotely and are opening up entirely remote roles every day.

This means that work seekers can extend the work quest to various cities and countries. You are not constrained by simple geography anymore, and you can easily find positions for which you are eligible.

Social Recruiting

Almost every company is on Facebook, Twitter, YouTube; it is not surprising that they use their social media to attract talent to their company. It is generally referred to as 'social recruitment', and you should pay attention to this growing phenomenon. You will follow the companies that you would like via different social media channels if you want to find a well-paying job. Many will post job openings in social media, and you will find a career appropriate for you.

Artificial Intelligence

Artificial intelligence (AI) is an essential part of many recruitment and talent acquisition aspects. Today, human and artificial intelligence work together to advance, which will potentially change the recruiting environment for the better. Chatbots are so smart that you hardly judge that you do not interact with a person. Eighty percentage of businesses are expected to use Chatbots by 2020 (Source: Chatbot Report 2019: Global Trends and Analysis). In the recruitment industry, we are beginning to see similar adoptions.

Since many years now, Chatbots have been in the recruiting field. Still, their use has been restricted to call for action at the landing page and invite candidates to apply. Today, however, Chatbots are being tested to schedule interviews.

These Chatbots entertain applicants in a human-sounding text conversation to collect responses, images, videos and documents. They are empathetic, compassionate and helpful and can be chatted, emailed or written.

The interview process has also changed by technology, with Skype interviews becoming more frequent. A study published in 2017 by Deloitte reported that 33 percentage of respondents have already used some form in their hiring processes, beginning with automated text or e-mails that confirm interviews, communicating basic needs and details (such as the beginning date and pay) via immediate messaging systems.

However, AI may be much more useful for the future of recruiting as more businesses continue to interview applicants via algorithmically enhanced video systems. For example, HireVue provides companies with an on-demand video interview platform for job seekers that evaluate the answers received with advanced machine learning. In order to complete a rounded profile of the applicant for hiring managers, the platform also focuses on facial expressions and preference. It eliminates the time needed to select potential applicants, and multiple interviews can be carried out in tandem, saving recruiters' hours.

Talent rediscovery software uses the ATS resume database to show candidates who have applied for a position. It then verifies that these applicants meet the current job specifications.

The technology will contact the candidates via social media or by e-mail, once the match is identified. It also scouts its social media accounts to check for potential positions and then adds them to the applicant profile.

Sixty-three percent of respondents said that AI had altered how recruitment took place in the company according to a Korn Ferry Global survey. Candidates not only have to pass human doorkeepers while they are applying for a new job but also have to rely on a rigorous test of artificial intelligence.

One Israeli start-up named VoiceSense analyses over 200 voice features and then builds user profiles by using the details. The next step is to decide which people suit the best based on the indications of vocal parameters.

There is an AI recruiting tool known as Knockri, which analyses the vocal and facial expressions. A technology representative says its company hires 17% more coloured people than conventional approaches, as well as more women. It ranks applicants without disclosing names and genders.

Future of Work

Job seekers should keep an eye on the dynamics changing the future of work. It is crucial to know the future of work and required skills. Technological and social powers are remodelling how businesses and organisation are working. Technology is performing its role to enhance productivity;

there will be a noteworthy disturbance as organisations wrestle with the complexity and unpredictability of a dynamic workforce.

Research by Deloitte Consulting reveals that seven potent disruptors are reshaping the future of work. To counter these disruptors, corporate leaders need to engage in creative thinking that can not only re-design but also re-imagine how businesses tackling jobs. They need to think big, focus on agility, and, eventually, to push faster than the new realities of work.

According to the World Economic Forum, the half-life of the skill has decreased from 30 years to an average of 6 years. It is applicable, not only for experienced professionals but also for fresh graduates. It means that the model of "learning at school" and "doing at work" is no longer sustainable. Lifetime learning and development will be a way of life at work. Reskilling is a top priority for organisations looking at their future employment strategy.

Individuals, companies and education sector must find joint and sophisticated solutions that work for everyone and must push for smart ways of promoting balance and revisionist thinking at work. Governments and policymakers can play a vital role in this new paradigm through bold leadership in education and labour market regulations. In addition, by developing standards that will enable and accelerate the future of work opportunities. A collective response should create opportunities that boost and allow people to reinvent themselves and begin on new directions and develop their careers.

Company leaders should no longer be passive users of ready-made human resources. They should consider talent management and development at the forefront and concentrate on their growth strategies. It takes a new approach to recognise the obstacles faced by workers and sketching talent initiatives and models that unlock their potential.

Source: Deloitte Consulting LLP and Deloitte Insights

Technology

Technology has flourished from gadgets to the Internet of Things (IoT), allowing utterly different working methods. Digital and technological skills are not crucial for the leaders but also for employees at every level.

Tsunami of Data

Today we have an explosion of information. Data has

grown into a tsunami. Organisations who want to promote growth in companies must leverage the power of big data and analytics.

Automation

An evolving "cyber-physical world" emerged that focuses on effectiveness and automation of manual tasks to reduce costs and keep up with the competitors. Organisations have introduced the concept of the digital factory, paperless work environment and fully automated work processes.

Jobs & Automation

Automation is affecting every industry and field of life. It generates new jobs with essential human abilities and an emphasis on creating higher values.

Change in Nature of Career

Technology has changed the meaning of "career," which acknowledges that extended life leads to working experience of 60-70 years with continued learning and career transitions.

Explosion in Contingent Work

Contingent work with a distributed pool of talent has exploded, increasing productivity and speed.

Diversity & Generation Change

Diversity and generational change make open dialogue, employee empowerment, and inclusion quite a common thing at the workplace.

Advancements in technology not only changing the way we

work, but also changing the design and structure of the organisations.

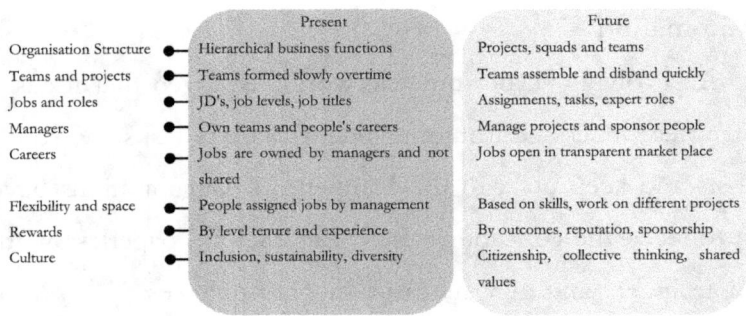

	Present	Future
Organisation Structure	Hierarchical business functions	Projects, squads and teams
Teams and projects	Teams formed slowly overtime	Teams assemble and disband quickly
Jobs and roles	JD's, job levels, job titles	Assignments, tasks, expert roles
Managers	Own teams and people's careers	Manage projects and sponsor people
Careers	Jobs are owned by managers and not shared	Jobs open in transparent market place
Flexibility and space	People assigned jobs by management	Based on skills, work on different projects
Rewards	By level tenure and experience	By outcomes, reputation, sponsorship
Culture	Inclusion, sustainability, diversity	Citizenship, collective thinking, shared values

Source: Deloitte Consulting LLP and Deloitte Insights

Organisation Structure

Today, many organisations have hierarchical structures based certain departments and levels. In a hierarchical organisation, workers are graded at different levels within the organisation, each level being one above the other. At each point of the chain, one individual has many employees directly under his influence. A large hierarchical organisation has many levels, and only a few will have a flat hierarchical organisation. The chain of command, i.e. how the authority is organised, is a typical pyramid shape.

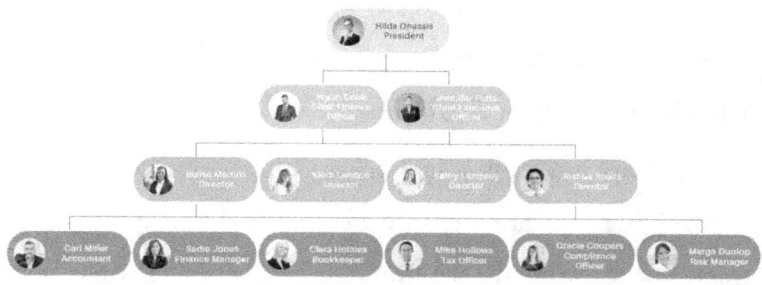

According to Deloitte Consulting, many organisations have already shifted away from functional structures. Just 38% of all businesses and 24% of large companies (> 50,000 employees) are still formally structured. The rise of millennial populations, the diversity of global teams, and the need to innovate and work more closely with customers are driving new organisational versatility among high-performing companies.

Organisations function as a network of groups within orthodox systems, with individuals shifting from team to team rather than staying in rigid hierarchical configurations.

Teams & Projects

In conventional organisations, teams formed slowly over the period to carry out specific projects while modern organisations enable people to move from team to team as needed. Similar to the way that expert come together for particular projects or global assignments. Then ensure that people have a home to go back to when a team-based project is completed. It will shift the definition of "job description" to that of "mission specialist" or "technical specialist."

Job Descriptions & Roles

Many organisations assign concrete job descriptions based on level and position. Future lies in fluid job descriptions, which focus more on assignments and tasks. People work together based on projects and assignments instead of having conventional job description because of certain position in an organisation. Which means, flow of talent across departmental boundaries and transfer of knowledge.

Managers and Careers

In a conventional organisation structure, managers control teams and people's career. Modern organisation transfers managers to positions that concentrate on planning, policy, vision, community, and cross-team communication. They will be responsible for managing projects and sponsoring people.

Flexibility and Space

Presently, people get assignments by the management while in future jobs shall be assigned based on skills and projects. Organisations focus on training and encouraging people to work crosswise teams like "hackathons," open office spaces that foster collaboration and job rotation to give teams a shared understanding of each other.

Rewards

Usually, conventional organisations reward people based on tenure in the company and experience level. Now organisations are focusing on optimising performance management around "team performance" and "team leadership" rather than concentrating solely on individual performance and assigning individuals as leaders only by their title or position. They are rewarding people for project outcomes, collaboration, and helping others.

Organisational Culture

Currently, organisational culture revolves around inclusion, sustainability and diversity. Future of work lies in corporate culture, which challenges the traditional organisational structures. It believes in enabling teams, holding people liable, and focus on developing a culture of shared information, accorded vision, and prevailing direction. Collective thinking, shared values and shared vision are the critical elements of an organisational culture of the future.

Top Eight (8) Skills for Future

In a dynamic work environment, especially during industry 4.0 revolution and now after the impact of COVID-19, it is essential to understand the critical skills that employees in both the private and public sectors. It does not matter you are a job seeker or already working. If you want to succeed in your future careers, you need to assure that you have the skills, which are in demand and valuable.

Overall, social skills, such as persuasion, emotional intelligence, and training others, will be more demanding than traditional technical skills, such as programming or administering and controlling machine. Nevertheless, technical skills will be essential for a stable job, career longevity and satisfaction.

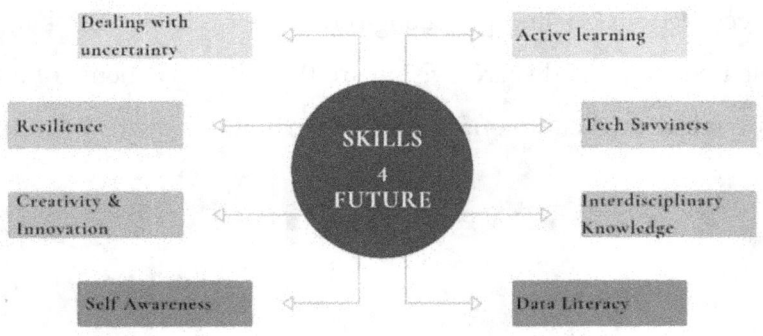

Source: WEF, Forbes, OECD 2019

Dealing with Uncertainty

In a continually changing world of work, you need this skill more than ever before. Just as other industrial revolutions transformed the skillset and experience required from the workforce, we can expect the same from industrial revolution 4.0. The ability to 'solve novel, ill-defined, multi-dimensional problems in complex, real-world settings.' Coping with a volatile, uncertain, complex and ambiguous world. Most of us view uncertainty as disruptive. In today's unpredictable world, you cannot avoid uncertain and ambiguous situations, so you have to learn to deal with vague conditions.

You can learn and unlock it by conditioning your mind to accept for change and prepare for every possible scenario. It would be best if you look at the bigger picture by channelizing the positive thinking. Think positive without over-thinking.

COVID-19 is the most prominent example of such a scenario, which is changing the dynamics all over. It has affected us personally and professionally. It is a lesson learned not for individuals but the corporate world as well.

Resilience

Resilience is a mind-set. It refers to how well you can cope with and recover from difficult situations. It also shows your ability to work under pressure and perform challenging tasks. It is the difference between staying calm under a perceived challenging situation and losing your coolness to the point of being out of control.

Resilient people tend to have a more optimistic attitude and to cope more effectively with stress.

You can increase your resilience by connecting with empathetic and understanding people. Sympathetic people can remind you that you are not alone in the middle of problems. Concentrate on getting dependable and compassionate individuals who endorse your feelings.

Foster wellness and find your purpose in personal and professional life to cope with the challenges.

Creativity and Innovation

Creativity is one of the essential desired skill in the future. Creativity is not the exclusive field of those in the arts. If you can connect the dots with apparently dissimilar data and launch all the ideas collectively to present something innovative, then you are a creative person.

Despite how many machines operate alongside us, humans are still more skilled at creativity. Creative humans are in high demand by companies to develop, visualise something novel and build a better future. Workplace of the future will necessitate new ways of thinking, and human creativity is critical to moving forward.

Self-Awareness

Self-awareness is the fundamental step of emotional intelligence. It guides how to recognise your sensations and emotions and be conscious of them, their triggers and their influence.

Another domain where humans have the advantage over machines is self-awareness and emotional intelligence. Our ability to be aware of, control, and express our emotions and the emotions of others. This skill will be valuable as long as there are humans in the workforce since it influences every cooperation we have with one another.

It helps us tune our emotions, and regulate how proficient we are at fixing our style depending on the state of a co-worker, or even our internal feelings.

Active Learning

Digital transformation, automation, fourth industrial revolution and constant technological change require re-skilling or up-skilling of the workforce continuously. Learning how to learn is crucial in this age of digitalisation and disruption.

Workplaces of the future require people with the ability to learn actively with a growth mindset. An individual with a growth mindset recognises that their capabilities and knowledge. They believe that learning can be expanded and they know their effort to develop skills will result in more significant accomplishment. They will, therefore, embrace challenges, learn from failures and actively explore disruption.

Tech Savviness

Workers will require technical skills in every industry since digital accessories will be common to perform every job. Artificial intelligence, IoT, virtual and augmented reality, robotics, and more will become a part of every worker's daily routine, whether the workplace is a manufacturing unit or consultancy firm. So, not only do individuals require to feel comfortable with these tools, they have to acquire skills to work with them. Recognition and understanding of these technologies and associated technical abilities will be required for every job.

On a more basic level, everyone requires to be able to realise the potential repercussions of new technologies on their industry, business, and job.

Interdisciplinary Knowledge

It requires linking the theories and concepts of one discipline or subject to the ideas and content of other disciplines or subjects. Interdisciplinary knowledge is increasingly critical for understanding and resolving complicated problems.

Classifying many resolutions to complex problems requires

thinking across disciplines, or "connecting the dots". An individual with interdisciplinary knowledge can think and propose innovative solutions and approaches, solve complicated intricacies using reasoning and logic and assess arguments.

Data Literacy

In a world propelled by data and information, professionals must develop strong data literacy capabilities. It illustrates the ability of an individual to recognise, interpret, elaborate, and use data.

Data has become a fuel in the digital journey of the organisations. Businesses that do not apply that ammunition to propel their success will unavoidably fall behind. Therefore, to make data relevant and valuable, and to create a competitive edge, organisations seek individuals who have data literacy and the skills to turn the data into business value.

Chapter Two

HUNT LIKE A PRO

It is so important to find a job, but it is time taking, confusing and cumbersome activity. The job search can feel overwhelming for many reasons. Probably you do not know where to start. Perhaps you have applied for many jobs online and could not get the opportunity to secure an interview. You are not sure what to do next, so you are going to focus on everything at once. Majority of the job seekers have no training to carry out a careful job search, and lack of required information about job transitions. You definitely cannot eat an elephant in one go, so better to cut the elephant in smaller pieces.

If you do not realise what you want or where you are heading, you have to redefine your method and refine your quest. You have applied for multiple roles and job opportunities, but nothing is working out. You are in a panic and tossing a big net trying to catch everything. What is going to happen is that there are not enough interviews and nobody is going to respond. I do not want you to make the mistake of free execution, of jumping out into the universe without a strategy.

Please take a sheet of paper. This is going to be a straightforward phrase, covering four elements, the qualities that you have to put on the table, the position, and the place, where you want to work. Tell yourself, which is the source of what you do best and what you like to do to describe your capabilities?

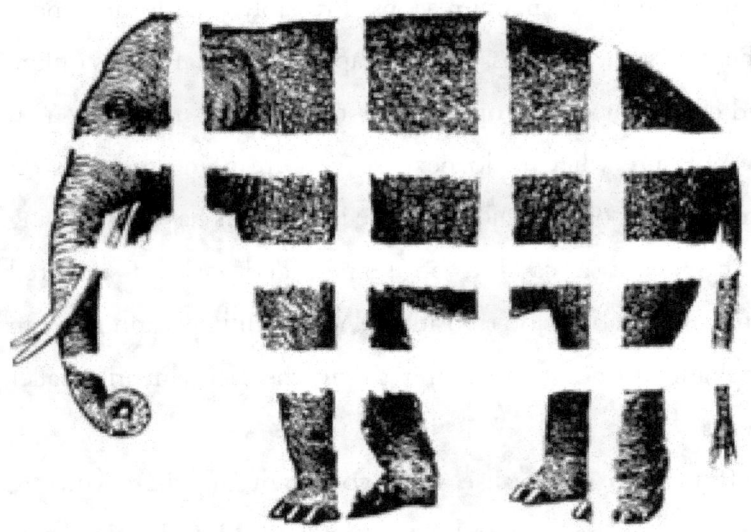

What are you trying to bring to your next work at the table? What kind of people has helped or complimented you on LinkedIn over the years? Think about the work that has to be finished. You may want to operate just remotely or with a limited amount of pay.

Firstly, make a long list here to figure out to make it clear what is most relevant to you. Secondly, decide on your trail. What is the right path of your journey? You have to kick off your expedition, are you ready to move? These great choices have an impact on your life. Your schedule is the answer. You can actively search for the next year, or you may need a job as early as possible. Understand how easily you are going to make a transition, as it will apply to your plan. You have to write down your goal, initiatives and everything else, which will lead you towards your destination. Writing it all down would help you to decide, which careers are right for you and what are your no go areas.

Craft a "Job Hunting Plan"

Let us get right to the coronary heart of one of the most critical errors job seekers make so you can keep away from it. Many times, when a person decides that they want to find a new job, they assume that the first step is to create or update their resume. Moreover, do not get me wrong, having an updated and compelling resume is incredibly vital. Nevertheless, having a proactive plan earlier than you get going will make every part of this phase so much easier. It will make it much less complicated on the way to position yourself as a strong fit if you recognise who you are.

It will additionally make it less complicated for you to create your overall plan. In addition, you will be able to define your goals, related deadlines, discover who could be your first-degree connections help you to network with the right people. What I mean to say, do not set off on this adventure tour of job hunting without a proper plan.

Use your goal as the guiding star in your job search. Now it is time to look at the condition of your job hunting tools. Go ahead and locate your resume, cover letter templates, and letters of recommendation, and then be sincere with yourself about the readiness and relevance of your material. Chances are they require fine-tuning and customisation. Identify the areas of improvement and customise them accordingly. Do not forget to define your timelines according to the activities involved in this process.

Evaluate your network critically and analyse your contribution. Relationships sustain because of meaningful give and take. So ask yourself, are you adding value to your network? Have you referred at least two people in your network to jobs in the past year? This is important because I believe that to get a job; you also need to open up connections for others. Next, I want to suggest you consider whether you have a group of trusted advisers and mentors, you can contact for career advice. Every person in your network has value to add, so build your network sensibly and add people from different industries, roles, and levels of experience.

You might have a professor from University, a mentor in your organisation. You might know a friend who works in a similar industry but at a different company.

Make sure to utilise the potential of your network and seek help form them. Do not forget to explore the potential of networking groups and events. No matter it's an alumni get-together, training event, industry-specific groups. Find out networking events in your surroundings and build professional connections, and do not forget to focus on meaningful contribution towards your network.

Remember, it is not all about taking favours; you need to give back to your network.

Now it's time to evaluate your digital footprint, which

means a careful analysis of your online presence, for example, presence on LinkedIn, Xing, Facebook, Twitter, profiles on all the relevant social media and job hunting platforms. Focus on your profile photo as you create or reactivate your profile on job hunting platforms.

Go through your account thoroughly and check out the relevance of your images, posts and other updates, and think if you want to share this information with potential employers. It is very useful to make a list of your dream employers to navigate your job hunting efforts in the right direction.

This list shall serve as guiding star and motivates you to keep the momentum high. After finalising the list of companies, follow their profiles on social media, connect with relevant people and contribute, if possible.

Now let us focus on all the important elements of job-hunting plan one by one.

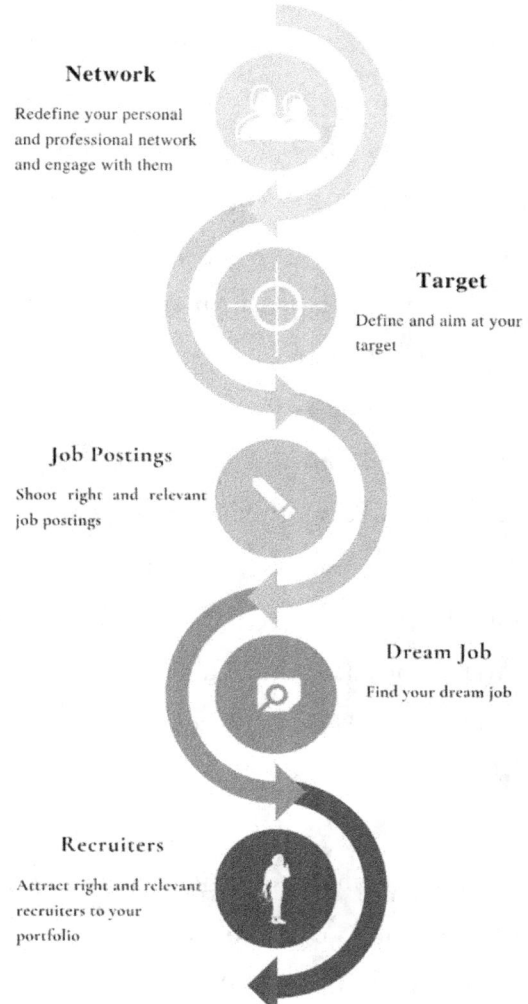

Network

Redefine your personal
and professional network
and engage with them

Target

Define and aim at your
target

Job Postings

Shoot right and relevant
job postings

Dream Job

Find your dream job

Recruiters

Attract right and relevant
recruiters to your
portfolio

Redefine Your Network

Next, look at your network. Evaluate your value addition towards your connections. Have you helped at least two people in your network to secure a job? This is important to me because I believe that to get a job; you want to open up contacts for others. Next, I would like you to consider whether you have a group of trusted mentors' advisers to seek career advice. Get their feedback.

Each person on your personal board should have a different approach, so you should look for people in the industry, roles and experience level. For example, you may find a college professor. You may find a mentor in your company. You might have a partner who works in a similar industry but at a different company. Use it as a counselling cabinet that guides you in the right direction in your career. Online or offline, whether you belong to any free or paid networking groups. It could be a meeting, it could be a chamber of commerce, or it could be industry-related.

Think about what kind of networking events you are bound to attend next month, and aim to get back to your network twice a week. It is time to evaluate your job hunting accounts on LinkedIn, Monster, Bayt and other job portals.

Check your social media accounts and ask yourself, are there any photos, feeds, and status updates you would like to show to a potential employer? Therefore, think of yourself as someone who is preparing relevant content on social media, and know that recruiters and hiring managers can access what you believe is private posts. Then list the dream companies you want to work with and why. This is a great list to keep you motivated. The thing is if you received a call from them, would you give up this offer. Once you know who these are for you, revisit these companies' sites regularly, looking at what jobs are available, noting where the company is headed. Moreover, take note of their press.

Engage Your Network

Inform at least five people in your network that you are seeking a job; you never know who is going to refer you somewhere. Remember, it does not matter how many people you know, what matters how many people know you. Your network can help speed up the process, but it can also be frustrating. Approaching your network is not easy. For some people, it is very complicated, and they do not do anything. While others do it the wrong way.

So how do you get people on your network to help you sincerely, what you are trying to achieve? First, let us think about the people you know best. It is surprising how many job seekers ignore the possible value of their family and friends. They are the ones who are likely to bend back for you.

Consider the professional contacts that you know pretty well, but maybe you have not spoken to them recently. Approach them, keep your post crisp and seek out their help and kindness. Create a bit of a rapport before you ask for any favour. Do not just ask them to handover over your resume to their boss.

Moreover, as a final point, think about your lost connections. I am talking about those people who were part of your network in the past. Maybe you have only met them once or twice. Do not be afraid to ask them, just do so in a very respectful way and respect the importance of their time.

In addition, do not forget to remind them about how you people know each other. Avoid big expectations and demands; inquire them if they would link you to someone relevant to the job you are searching.

In short, the secret to powerful networking is to be pure and concise, courteous, and make it super simple for them to say yes.

Aim At Your Target

When you dive into a job hunt, one of the most critical stuff you can do is to define the exact destination you want to land. If you go for everything, it would be tough to grab something. It is a lot easier, if you focus on a bunch of different things, to create an impactful curve, LinkedIn profile or game plan at once. You would also find it much harder to allocate precious time on so many things or initiatives simultaneously.

Focus on the activities, which will reinforce the process of job searching effective and efficient, and increase the quantum of your search. Yet having a primary point of focus will make the job search simpler. It will also help you develop a resume that speaks directly to the type of employment you like and want to live.

So let us look at a couple of fast tricks that will help you narrow down on the work.

Next, move over to LinkedIn and click on jobs. If you are in this area, enter some of the keywords and skills you want to use.

For now, do not think about the location. The aim of this is to make you research the goals and objectives and titles of the jobs you are most attracted to.

For example, maybe you are a very powerful problem solver with a finance background, and you are speaking German, you can use this information to search for relevant jobs. You are likely to see finance and accounting related jobs, particularly those serving a multilingual client base. Second, once you have this, save the job requirements that you believe are better suited to the next role you want. Try three to five job descriptions.

Now, take the highlighter and lay it down side by side. Where are the most frequent coinciding requirements? You might see yourself good in team leadership, proven success in developing new markets, and the ability to handle a broad range of customers.

Hence, assuming that you are a successful leader who has developed new regions and can carry out a considerable workload. You need to make that very clear in your resume, in your LinkedIn profile and every other channel you are using to market yourself professionally. You will also be able to see what the next job could be named if you are not sure about it yet. Trust me; this is going to make it a lot easier for you while you continue to fine-tune your career quest.

Shoot Right Job Postings

Seeking jobs that are significant for you is crucial. Many job seekers who are tired because they spend several hours a day, randomly searching the job boards every single day. I am not suggesting this approach. If you are going to use the job boards, you should be careful and strategic. Find only a handful that best serves your needs, your sector, and your goals.

First, start with LinkedIn. Do you know that LinkedIn also has a phenomenal jobs section that allows you to apply across the platform? Additionally, it tells you who works on the company in your network, which is super convenient. LinkedIn also helps you to set up reminders based on your current career goals.

Focus on industry-specific job portals. You will find unique sites for a specific industry. You can just use Google search, such as job boards for Engineers, and you will find a variety of choices. Do not forget to check out the regional job boards, which are very useful if you want to perform your search at a specific location.

Finally yet importantly, do not forget to define your dream employers and periodically check their websites, company pages on social media platforms, especially career pages. Be careful about the positions you are applying for because even though this is your dream employer, no one wants you to apply for irrelevant positions in the same company. Be diligent, be pragmatic, and find the best jobs for you.

Find Your Dream Job

It has never been easier to engage with prospects than digging LinkedIn or Google, checking industry job boards, and networking with past and present colleagues. The primary objective, while you are looking for jobs, is to get back to your job-hunting goal.

So be vigilant, search for keywords that are related to your skills. Look for areas where you would be able to stay and work. Check the websites of your dream employers every couple of months. Make sure you do not miss the perfect position just because you have seen a post too late.

Social media is yet another perfect way to find employment. In addition to LinkedIn, check Twitter, Facebook, Instagram and YouTube. You can follow your favourite organisations, and you can do hashtag searches for desired opportunities.

Digitally advanced companies putting together creative video resume competitions or innovative job descriptions that are shareable and enjoyable. In other words, employers are embedding the element of fun and gaming in their recruitment process. Remember that networking is by far the most effective way to find a new role. Many vacancies go unpublished because internal or chosen applicants are in the pipeline.

About 70% of positions are filled by network referrals, making it one of the most critical and valuable methods you can consider in your job hunt. Invest in your network today so that tomorrow, if you have a demand, it is abundant and equipped.

It means communication and cooperation with people, giving insightful information to others when they need help, and exchanging useful content with people you meet.

Attract Right Recruiters

It is vital to have the ability to apply efficiently for jobs that you find posted online. Things will not work if you just apply for jobs, then sit back, and relax. If that is the only way you are looking for a career, you could be in for a long time. Instead of depending on a mechanism that pits you against a bunch of other blind applicants, try weaving with some more useful strategies. For example, you might enlist the help of agency recruiters employed in your industry. You may refine your LinkedIn profile to attract the right recruiters.

Ensure to toggle on the LinkedIn notification that informs the recruiters that you are open for new opportunities. You can find this by clicking the Jobs tab, clicking career preferences, and then enabling this feature. Nevertheless, you do not have to hang around to be discovered, you can reach them directly. Now, this strategy is going to work better if you do some research first. You do not want to reach out to recruiters who do not fill the kind of positions you are looking for.

It might be intimidating because they might not react to you. Well, it works, but do your homework, ask people who work in similar positions if they are using a recruiter and who they would suggest. Observe the job ads you see posted online by the recruitment agencies. If that organisation has one job related to your profession, they may very well be skilled in that industry. You will also be able to contact the local branch of your professional association. They are very likely to be aware of the best recruiters in your region.

Moreover, if everything else fails, please use the multidimensional Google. You will definitely find a few companies that could be a good match. You can start with search terms like Finance recruiters in Dubai or Mumbai executive search firms. Feel free to contact them directly. You do not challenge or bargain with them to take you on or do any great favour for you.

HACK A Job

Unemployment is increasing across the globe with a high pace due to lack of employment opportunities, economic slow-down, rising number of graduates in the market, especially after COVID-19 crises.

Getting a job is not an easy task due to fierce competition. You cannot merely apply for the job; literally, you have to HACK the job. Nevertheless, that is easier said than done. You have to demonstrate a high level of patience and persistence.

What does HACK mean? I am not advising you to hack the career portals of the companies or recruitment agencies.

HUNT
It's natural but technical to chase a job. Your knowledge, skills and abilities must be understood to look for jobs that suit your profile and expertise.

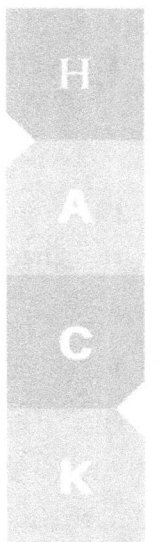

APPLY
Apply only for relevant vacancies. Word "relevant" is integral; you should not apply to the jobs beyond your skillset; otherwise, you will only waste your precious time.

COMMUNICATE
Communication will definitely help you to get yourself on the interview table if you meet the job requirements. Effective Communication is the key to success.

KEENNESS
During your communication or interaction with the recruiters or potential employers, show your keenness, enthusiasm and motivation to join them.

i.   Hunt

Hunting a job is natural but technical. You have to understand your knowledge, skills and abilities to search for suitable jobs according to your profile and skillset. Companies publish their vacancies on various platforms like Newspaper Advertisements, Career portals, LinkedIn and other social channels.

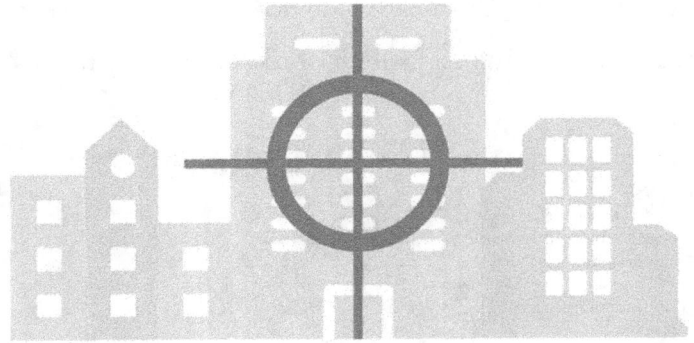

Beware, many jobs also go unannounced, so you have to be very thorough and professional in your research about the employment market. Tap your network and connect with people. Many people in your existing network may have vacancies relevant to you but never thought about you. Try to list down all of your contacts and set a goal to initiate communication with them and let them know about your availability for a career move.

Identify the decision-maker and source of information and strengthen your professional relationship with them. Many candidates fail to conduct proper research due to lack of awareness and knowledge. Connect with alumni; we generally like those who are like us. Grow your network by attending alumni events and strengthen your relationship with peers and seniors. Maximise the use of LinkedIn to get maximum information about companies and upcoming jobs. Connect with the HR Professionals and potential managers, working in the industry that suits you.

ii. Apply

Do not just shortlist and apply for the vacancies based on position titles, go through the job descriptions in detail and compare it with your resume. Please apply only for relevant vacancies. Word "relevant" is integral, you should not apply to the jobs beyond your skillset; otherwise, you will only waste your precious time. Before you send out any applications, you should do a little work on your online reputation to make sure it is up to hiring managers' par. You should carefully update your profiles on social media platforms like LinkedIn. Go through the employer's website; get information about their business process, company culture, organisational values and other relevant aspects. After careful research about the organisation and the job, if you really think that you are the perfect candidate for this role, apply.

iii. Communicate

After searching and applying for the relevant vacancies, now you have thrown the ball in the court of the recruiters. Recruiters may or may not shortlist you for the interview phase due to the high number of applicants. If you are confident that you fulfil all the requirements of the role, do not sit back and relax, and wait for your turn. Try to find out some connections within that company, get in touch with the recruitment team. Push your connections to arrange a face-to-face interview so that you could prove your metal.

In case you do not find any connections within your network, try to talk or meet the recruiters directly. Try to get feedback about your employment application. Believe me; this communication will definitely help you to get yourself on the interview table if you meet the job requirements. Effective communication is the key to success. Please communicate with the recruiters or employers during the office hours, try to respect their personal life.

iv. Keenness

During your communication or interaction with the recruiters or potential employers, show your keenness, enthusiasm and motivation to join them.

Keep in mind the difference between keenness and desperation. Employers and recruiters should not get the impression that you are desperate for the job, your distress may result in an adverse reaction. Employers may exploit your desperation in many ways.

Chapter Three

ULTIMATE RESUME

Some organisations are moving to use more creative or digital platforms rather than a traditional resume or CV. However, these organisations are still in the (relative) minority. Nevertheless, many companies rely on a traditional resume or CV as a tool for initial shortlisting.

So, work on your resume or CV to ensure that it represents you in the best possible way. Draft a master copy of your document, containing all the experience, education, training and competencies. Later on, you can customise your piece of paper based on the job. Do not forward the same document for every job. Always remember that one size does not fit all. Aim your resume or CV to win a job interview, some people have a misconception that a resume or CV will get you a job, they completely misunderstand the role of this vital document.

A hiring manager will never offer a candidate a position just by reading the resume. Companies only use them to decide to shortlist the candidates for the interview phase.

A resume or CV is there to win you an interview, and you should write it by keeping this objective in mind. "Your resume must explain effectively and precisely of your worth as a potential contributor to the success of the organisation. You should provide clear, concise and easily digestible information that could help the recruiter to understand your value instantly. Recruiters usually spend seconds to skim through your resume. The resume or CV takes you only the first few paces toward that new job. It gets you a place on the interview table, and because you can't be there to answer questions, it has to stand on its own."

Customisation of resume or CV is critical, but you have to be very careful. Recruiters can tell when a document is standard or customised, as it will include information that is redundant for the job in question.

Resume VS CV

Primarily the main differences between a resume and a CV are the length, what is included. Nevertheless, both are used in job applications, a resume and a CV are not always interchangeable. CV delivers a snapshot of your education, work experience, skills and competencies. Typically, CVs are detailed than resumes - at least two or three pages, containing information about your academic background, experience, training, certifications, presentations, publications and other achievements.

A resume shows the summary of your educational background, work experience, certifications, job-related skills and competencies. There are likewise discretionary segments, including a resume objective and career synopsis articulation. Resumes are the most widely recognised document mentioned of candidates in employment applications. A resume ought to be as concise as could be expected under the circumstances.

Typically, a resume is one page long, albeit occasionally it tends to be up to two pages. Often resumes include to the point information in the bulleted form to keep information concise. Resumes come in a few types, including chronological, functional, and combination formats. Select a format that best fits the kind of job you are applying for.

The summary is a one-to-two-page, overview or compact and brief version. It is a way to convey one's skills and qualifications, precisely and concisely. Sometimes large organisations will ask for a one-page summary when they expect a large pool of applicants. While writing a resume, it is vital to keep in mind that a recruiter does not read it thoroughly. They quickly go through and scan them for aspects that match the profile they are searching for. According to research, a recruiter takes two to three minutes on average to judge a letter and CV or resume. Therefore, ensure that your cover letter or resume is capable of convincing in those few minutes.

Employers receive many resumes for a job, which has been advertised, so it is crucial to leave a good impression to attract their attention. Most people do not spend the required time on their resume, so if you write a professional, high-quality document, you will definitely stand out from the rest.

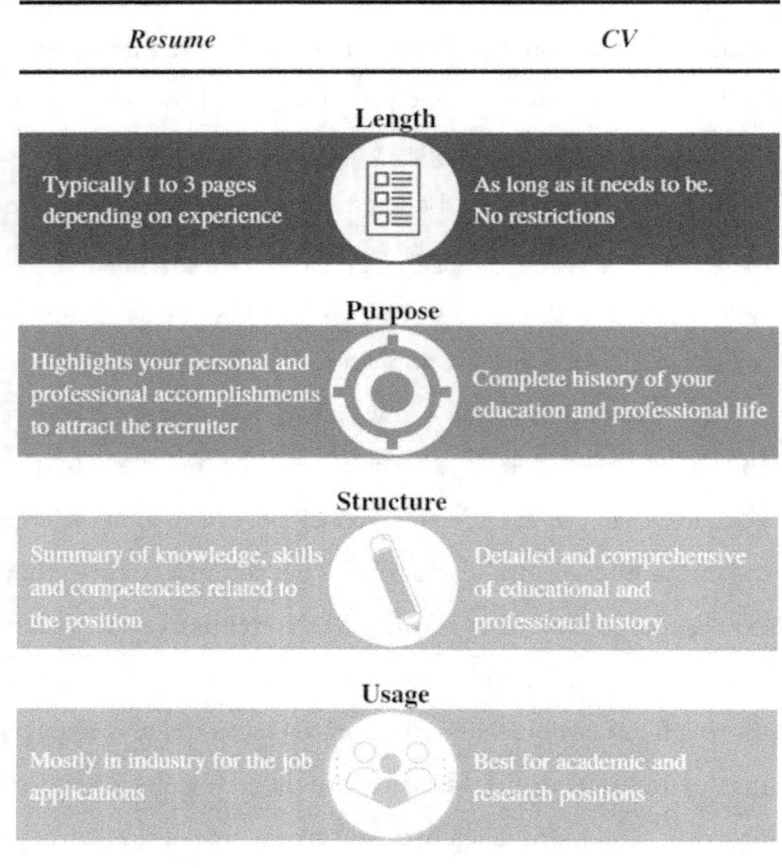

Resume	*CV*
Length	
Typically 1 to 3 pages depending on experience	As long as it needs to be. No restrictions
Purpose	
Highlights your personal and professional accomplishments to attract the recruiter	Complete history of your education and professional life
Structure	
Summary of knowledge, skills and competencies related to the position	Detailed and comprehensive of educational and professional history
Usage	
Mostly in industry for the job applications	Best for academic and research positions

Knock-Down ATS

What would you do to boost your resume while applying for online jobs to bypass this irritating porter known as ATS? Simply put, "Applicant Tracking System" is a software, which firms and recruiting companies use to store, sort and eventually select applicants. It is essentially a massive database for searchable recipients to identify so-called best-suited applicants for roles or tasks.

When you apply for a position by submitting your resume to an online site, there is a fair chance that a person will not check your documents first. Your employment application will be reviewed by ATS. If ATS decides that you are a good fit for further consideration, you can move on to the human eyeballs. So, let us break down the critical stuff to make a difference by improving your ATS resume.

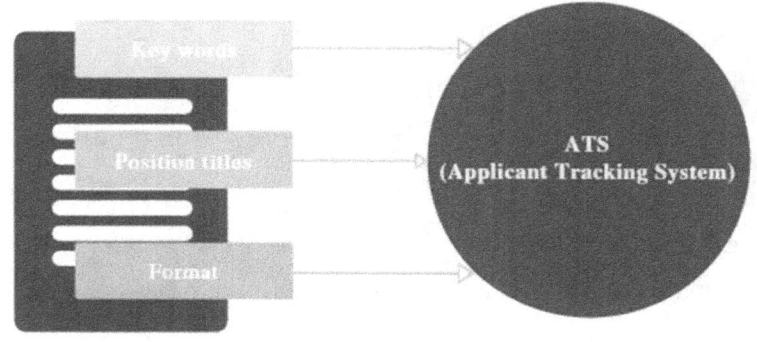

| Tips to knock-down ATS and increase the chances |

i.   Keywords

You must match your resume with the job description. Look for keywords that are used regularly and prominently in the job description, and make sure to include them in your resume. Those are the same words that the recruiter would use when looking for the best-matched applicants.

ii.   Position titles

If you are an HR Specialist, whose current title is a Happiness Officer or something super arbitrary? You better describe yourself as an HR Specialist so that the ATS knows you are in line with that work. In short, the title of your position should be universal rather than unique or company-specific. Remember that position titles vary from company to company.

iii.   Format

Keep it smooth and clear, as if you are not going nuts with a lot of columns, headers, odd fonts, and graphics. Any of these may interrupt the parsing process. Moreover, in the worst case, you may be the most eligible person on earth, but if your knowledge parses the ATS as a grim mess, you will not turn up as a strong match. Use standard desktop fonts, such as Arial, Garamond, and Calibri. Finally, avoid using a functional resume or one that shows your entire career highlights and skills first-hand without tying them to the corresponding position. Use a reverse-chronological format or a hybrid format instead.

"I think I'm most interested in hearing about the part of your resume titled 'Stuff I Totally Rocked.'"

Cover Letter

Cover letters have become a thing from history. Some of the applicant tracking systems do not even demand you to add one or make it discretionary. It is nice to have a cover letter if you are willing to make an effort to customise it for every job. It is very tempting to write a cover letter full of claims.

Introduce yourself politely and then demonstrate your understanding and knowledge about the position you are applying for. Prove that you know what the organisation is up to, and you know what the problems this work is going to solve.

Speak about why you are the best person on the planet to carry out the job responsibilities effectively and efficiently.

Crafting an "Ultimate Resume"

There are thousands of templates and as many tips on how to do it well. I will focus on three common types: chronological, practical, and hybrid or composite.

The first type of resume is chronological or sequential. Sometimes it is also called the reverse chronological resume. It focuses heavily on the roles that you have played and the duration of each one. If you have mostly played the same business and position and have a steady job history, you will find it an excellent choice. It is also the favourite of the employer. It gets to the point quickly, you cannot read much before you get there and it is really aimed at your positions and each one's responsibilities.

The other resume type is functional. If you have significant gaps in your job history, that is great. Let us say you had an unemployment period of a year or two, or maybe you took some time to go to school or to go to the family. It lists the selected experience, which is vital for a role in the functional resume. Here you see a summary of who you are as a professional. A breakdown of your work by focusing more on your skills than on positions and tasks in detail. This is, therefore, a way to highlight the spotty deficiencies in your history. The job is still down there and has dates, but it is not so prominent. Now, a word of warning, employers are not always the most significant fans of functional type, because they want to play down the work history and experience.

The third type is the hybrid that combines chronological as well as functional elements. This resume has an overview, which we saw from the functional one. Still, your experience is included so that can quickly show your work history and associated tasks. Education, professional training and skills, are listed at the end.

If you want to show how your skills and work can be translated, this is an intelligent choice. The best time to update your resume is if your career gains are significant. When you finish that important project on time, get an award or move to a new department while everything is fresh in mind. I would like to recommend that you review it every four months with updates on any education, job expansions and recent victories you have completed. Calendar it, too, is a good practice.

| Ingredients of a winning resume |

Basic Structure of Resume

Regardless of which resume format you use, you need to include appropriate information written in a professional way that sells your expertise to the employer. It is incredibly significant to ensure the quality of your resume. The general presentation and layout, grammar, and most importantly, content require great attention. In the case of grammatical errors and mistakes, chances are quite high that employers will not even bother to read your document.

i. Name & Contact Details

It all starts with your name and contact information. Make sure to write the phone number and email, which are functional and you use frequently. Otherwise, you may miss an opportunity due to invalid contact details.

You should always put your full name (first and last) according to your legal documents, e.g., passport or driving license, at the top of each page. You can also include your middle name or initial if you prefer. Experts do not recommend writing nicknames, which do not sound professional. You may write your full and updated mailing address for any expected correspondence.

Mention your preferred phone number with country and area code for employers and recruiters to contact you, and ensure that you have a professional and polite voicemail greeting if you are unable to answer the phone. Most of the employers contact the job seeker through email, so ensure that you write a professional email in your resume. You should never mention funny email addresses like cute_boy@email.com, pretty_girl@email.com might leave a wrong impression. Always try to generate an email address based on your full name.

ii.   Nationality & Work Permit (optional)

In case you are applying for an overseas opportunity, you should write about your nationality, work visa status and other necessary details. This information is essential for the recruiters to check your eligibility to work in a specific country. Some countries have implemented nationalisation policies, which restrict expatriates to work in particular positions.

iii.   Career Objective or Summary

This section is the most critical element, which describes your purpose for the job. This statement assists employers in determining whether your objective is in line with the organisation goal and the position available. You should take time to draft a great beginning of your resume carefully. This section reveals your objectivity and long-term career aspirations.

In the past, most job seekers included a career objective on their resumes to tell hiring managers and recruiters, what type of position they were looking for. The latest trend is to add a summary statement or a personal profile in place of the objective. However, you may include both depending on the requirement of the position you want to apply.

These days some job seekers do not include specific career objective and keep it more general. The trend to ignore the career objective originates from recent research that shows you have a better chance for the interview if you write your resume to help an employer fill the open position according to their assessment, instead not to tell the employer what you want.

However, many job seekers still include it along with a professional summary, especially if they are new to the workforce. Note that whether or not employers expect to see a career objective on your resume is partly dependent on your field. In some areas, like education, job applicants are still likely to include an objective.

The personal profile/summary and profile statement do the same thing. It reaffirms merely the critical points of your resume, usually in a short paragraph or a few bullet points. It not only highlights the strategic points, but it often focuses more on your accomplishments and honours.

To be honest, it is entirely up to you to decide which works best for your resume considering your professional experience, skills, level of position, and qualifications for the job for which you are applying. By writing, an objective on your resume is a way to convince employers that you know about your job aspirations, while a profile describes what you have to offer the employer and can help sell your application. Another choice is not to use either and simply start resume with recent experience.

iv.   Work Experience

If you are an experienced professional, significant content in your resume is work experience. I would instead call it as power content; it will provide a boost to your profile. As a recruiter, I would shortlist the profile based on relevant experience. Irrelevant experience straightforwardly leads to disqualification. Do not forget to mention your position, tenure, organisation and brief job responsibilities, but focus on projects, assignments and achievements. Many candidates do not mention the accurate start and finish dates, which is wrong.

Majority of people write their work experience in chronological order and list the most recent and most relevant first. If you would instead write a skills-based resume, divide your employment profile into themes. The most important part is the list of your duties/responsibilities, so take your time over describing those. You want to tailor them for each job you apply for because you are trying to show that your experience from previous jobs makes you ideal for this one.

If you are a fresh graduate and lack prior experience, do not underestimate the power of internships and again, depending on the field you are looking to get into. Still, generally, I would say that internships are only going to add value to your application. Ideally, these internships will be directly related to the job you are looking to get into, but do not despair if not.

Some internships are really hard to get (I'm sure everyone wants to go and do an internship at Google or Facebook, but places are hard to come by), so if you can translate the experience you get in other intern roles to the permanent job you're applying for, it should still add value. If you have done jobs, you feel are irrelevant. For example, working in a restaurant or fuel station or in a shop will have given you the chance to display leadership skills, teamwork, customer orientation, negotiation skills and business development. You may also quote volunteer work as it depicts your commitment and passion. Do not undermine the value of transferable experience on your resume. You never know its worth.

v.   Achievements

They should match and correlate with your responsibilities. It shows that you were able to improve practically and personally the business of the company. You really contribute towards the success of the business and support the management to achieve the organisational goals. This section should not be blurred and general but specifically crisp, to-the-point and focused. If you worked in Sales, do mention the numbers, your annual target, order intake and sales achievement. Write about the projects that you completed with the project timeline. Do not take it for granted and do not be modest or under-market yourself. Brand yourself effectively to create a vibrant wavelength. Try to get perspective out of your experience and convert it into sellable content.

vi.   Accentuate Your Strengths

Almost every candidate highlights his/her strengths (i.e. communication skills, teamwork, and creativity) but does not back these up with real-world examples or solid evidence. There is a tendency from many organisations to use competencies to score applications or candidates in an interview. You should use these competencies to highlight your strong areas. Still, crucially you should support your claim ("I have great communication skills") with evidence ("I lead a project with a diverse team and utilise my cross-cultural communication skills"). Ideally, within reason, try to make this evidence/example as vivid as possible. In essence, you need to paint a picture that the reader can see. For example, you could also say you have "effective communication skills developed through regular presentations, written reports and case studies during college or university, resulting in first-class grades." Just remember that employers are interested in the outcome or impact of your actions, not just a list of the tasks themselves. Do not over-do this though – there is no point making up evidence or experience that you do not have. You will run the risk of being picked apart at the interview, and it will be embarrassing. Focus on the strengths you do have, make them as applicable to the job you are going for. If you've got enough evidence then you'll get an interview – if you don't, then maybe it's back to the drawing board to get more experience for next time around.

vii.   Educational History

Recruiters and Hiring Managers are also keen to know the qualifications of the candidates. Start with the last and most recent qualification. List your educational degrees or qualifications in reverse chronological order. Among the most important details is the name of the university or college that you attended. Your field of study and focus area or specialisation must be included, along with the title of your thesis and the final grade.

viii.   Professional Certifications

If you are a certified professional and hold accreditation from recognised institutes (i.e. CHRP, GPHR, SPHR, PMP, Programming, SAP, CIPD etc.) mention such qualifications. Remember that professional certification shows your commitments towards continuous professional development and put your profile in the spotlight.

It's worthy of adding an extra section on your resume to state professional certifications and licenses, as it is really beneficial in making your candidacy stand out in the screening process. Whether you have a long academic career with several degrees, or vocational or technical courses that have resulted in professional certificates or you have completed specific projects with your employer, which have given you a certain recognisable title, e.g. Certified Welder, Certified Draftsman etc. There are many ways to include certifications to attract the hiring manager's attention.

Certifications and additional qualifications exhibit an enthusiasm for the business or position of an applicant as give proof of explicit mastery and abilities. Professional licenses are indispensable to incorporate to give proof of your appropriateness to the position; mainly if these are, prerequisites referenced part of the expected set of responsibilities.

Constructing a winning resume can be a test for some job seekers and finding the ideal approach to incorporate certifications is necessary for specific occupations, regardless of whether the candidate is looking for an entry-level position or is applying for a comparable post to the one already held.

Firstly, applicants should assess their different certificates and decide whether each certificate is relevant and vital, or worth to add. Some job seekers will have many certifications to mention while others lack additional qualifications. That is why it is crucial to decide, which certifications are appropriate, to avoid unnecessary details.

You should distinguish between what should be included in a certificates section and what should be considered as honours and awards. Keep in mind that particular projects, assignments or accomplishments may have awarded you a certificate. Still, they are not professionally recognised certifications or licenses issued by legal bodies. Consider the job description for the position you are applying as standard and align this section based on job requirements.

Whereas, many applicants simply add appropriate certifications in other resume sections such as education or professional training. How to mention the certifications on a resume can also depend on the value of each qualification and requirements of the position. Better to include this section after the academic information.

ix.   Professional Trainings

A brief overview of relevant technical, behavioural, functional or leadership training history is worthy of mentioning. It shows the recruiter or hiring manager that you have built a theoretical base and enhanced your skills and competencies.

COMMOM MISTAKES TO AVOID

Your resume must be ideal, free of grammatical errors. If not, employers will read and draw less flattering conclusions about you, such as: "This person can't write," or "Obviously, this person is not caring."

1. Whenever you try to create an all-in-one resume for all employers, always something may be irrelevant. Employers want you explicitly to write a resume for them. You need to explain precisely how and why you fit in a specific organisation. For each job application, you do not have to thoroughly dissect or dismantle your resume. However, you have to modify your resume to match any job you are applying for.

2. For what you can read or hear, the length of your resume has no exact guidelines. Since people with different tastes and aspirations in terms of abstracts are reading it. This does not mean that, of course, you will begin to submit five-page resumes. Usually, you have to restrict yourself to two pages maximum. However, do not say that if you are going to use two sheets. Conversely, literally do not cut off your meat to adhere to an arbitrary norm of one paragraph.

3. Hiring managers read the objective statement of your resume. Still, so many times, they plough through the standard sets of the word, such as "To look for a challenging role that will bring professional development." Example: "A demanding marketing role in beginner level that enables me to contribute my expertise and experience in non-profit fundraising."

4. If a recruiter reads the same words or phrases, in summary, it becomes repetitive. It might also seem as if you were not cautious enough to use the action-oriented terms and to be precise to each position.

5. You can, for instance, be tempted to do nothing about the jobs you took to earn additional school money. However, the soft skills you have learned from these encounters are usually more important than you realise for employers.

6. If your resume has five different fonts in wall-to-wall texts, the employer will probably be afflicted with a headache. Before sending it out, reveal your document to your trustworthy friends and mentors. Do you find it appealing visually? When your eyes are hard to do, watch out.

7. Always double check your contact details before sending out your resume. Minute error, false contact details may cost you a job interview.

8. Remember those who made fun of yourself for not being "original" at school, college or university because of your email address. Your email address should represent you, not a Hollywood personality or a video game character. You do not want a hiring firm to neglect your expertise because he or she has been stuck in an email address called "fancy.hottie."

9. You will probably get your summary in the trash if your resume provides information that is outdated or irrelevant. Do not add your age, interests, or marital status into your resume that unless mentioned as a prerequisite. May lead to disqualification based on discrimination on issues like age and gender. Usually, it does not belong to the resume unless it applies to the work.

10. Show them the beauty of numbers. A recruiter wants to see the results in past positions. Results can be better represented as tangible results, the number of business growth, improved retention figures, increased profits, demonstrated investment return, etc. It might seem that you have "responsibilities." Still, you did not take any action or have real outcomes without displaying or presenting quantifiable results.

11. It is essential to include keywords from the work posting in your description. However, make sure that you intelligently add keywords. It will be painfully clear to the recruiter, to say no to a significant turnoff if you deliberately add keywords to your resume or use a set of annoying buzzwords. Using and incorporate keywords into your resume wisely, so they flow naturally and meaningfully. Consider anyone else reading your resume and see if some of your keywords are unforgiving.

Chapter Four

JOB HUNTING VIA LINKEDIN

No doubt, LinkedIn is the most powerful tool for job seekers and employers as of today. LinkedIn profile is your competitive advantage and a platform to display your knowledge, skills and abilities to the relevant people even in this era of fierce competition.

If you already have an account, you can experience that it is easy to highlight your talent, connect with recruiters and follow your favourite companies. In addition, it offers a lot of learning and career advice from experienced professionals.

It is the primary and most effective platform to find instant profiles. It helps the hiring managers and recruiters to avoid advertising an open role, but also to find "passive job-seekers" on LinkedIn. (You are not looking for them, so they are looking for you.) Of course, you do not have much influence on how they find you. Nevertheless, to make sure that you have a fully filled profile. They are searching by keywords.

Powerful LinkedIn Profile

If you do not have a profile, get on your laptop, connect to the internet and create a profile. Come on, let us create or optimise your LinkedIn profile together.

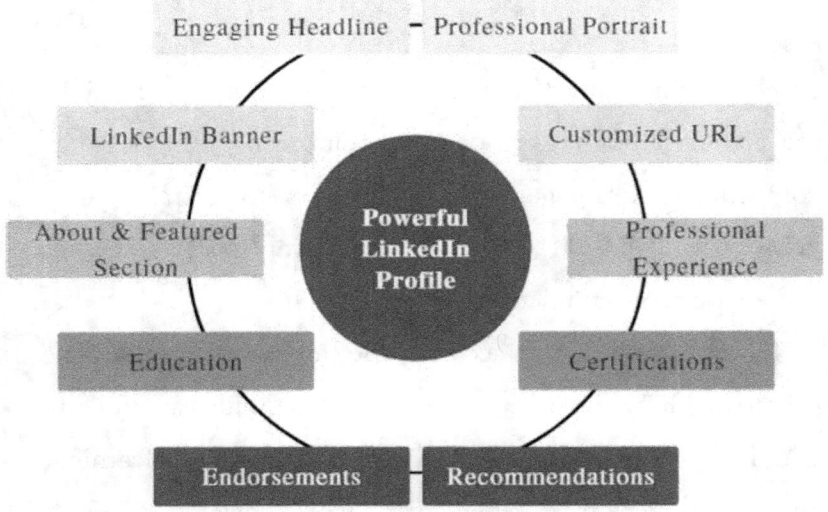

i.   Engaging Headline

Let us start with a compelling and attractive headline, which will be precisely under your name. By the way, write your full name. You should write an eye-catching headline that fascinates people's attention in you and describes who you are and what you do. There are many ways to do a headline right; focusing on either the value you can add or the role, you are performing. For examples, check out the headlines written by top industry professionals and LinkedIn influencers. Do not forget that is how you want recruiters to perceive you. Do not neglect to make it engaging, inspiring and relevant to your portfolio. Of course, there is no right or wrong, but experiment with different options and get feedback from career advisers, colleagues or peers before you decide. Remember to fine-tune, update and tweak it over time. Keep track of your profile views, and notice how many people are viewing your profile as your update and experiment with different headlines. You will get a clue about what is working.

ii.   Professional Photo

Get a professional portrait picture or use an image, which looks decent as your profile photo. Upload a recent photo preferable a headshot of just you so that if you engage in person with recruiters, they can effortlessly recognise you in a crowd. According to research, you are 11 times more likely to be viewed and considered genuine if you have a profile photo. Avoid uploading pictures that you have taken in events like marriage photos, party photos or other private events. Remember, that LinkedIn profile picture should be recent and realistic as it represents you as a professional.

iii.   Background Image or Banner

I suggest you to utilise all the available functionalities and tools provided by LinkedIn to optimise your profile. Many people ignore the background image, but you should select a background image that strengthens your image as a professional. It may be about your professional, interests or hobbies. Try to be creative and come up with an attractive and memorable image. It is an agile and practical way to set you apart quite quickly.

iv.   Customised URL

To make your LinkedIn portfolio more practical and personal, claim your customised URL. You can choose your full name, if available. Otherwise, try some other options, but keep it professional and accessible. It is definitely a convenient way to copy the link and add it on your resume and for recruiters to find you, much faster than a URL with random letters.

Navigate to your LinkedIn profile by simply clicking your profile picture. The extreme right, in the upper right corner, you will find the option of "Edit public profile & URL". Once you click this, a new window will open. Again in the extreme right side, in the upper right corner is your current profile URL. Notice that by default, the end of the URL will contain random numbers or letters. To customise this and create a personalised and unique URL, click on the pencil icon. Enter your full name or characters of your choice and click save.

v.   About & Featured Section

The most important thing, which you should never forget on your profile, is a compelling and convincing summary. According to research, your summary increases the chances of visibility 10 times. The summary section is the best place to brand yourself as a unique candidate. Create a sketch of your portfolio, elaborate your strengths, and focus on the value that you can add to the potential employers. Express your vision as an individual or professional and highlight your talents precisely and accurately.

Consider the profile summary as your elevator pitch. It should be an authentic prelude to you that is compact, elaborate your objective, impulse, essential talents and your experience. It is the best section to use keywords so people, especially recruiters, can locate you with ease and comfort. Make sure you display your career achievements and ambitions. Think of your profile summary as an introduction to who you are, what you do, why what you do matters, and the contribution you want to make or impact you want to have. Focus on storytelling; write an impressive and compelling story, which could represent you completely.

Let me tell you with a guarantee that your profile summary is the primary section recruiters view while visiting your profile. That is why it is essential to use your summary as a chance to present yourself and highlight your unique skills, impulses, and expertise. Ideally, a summary of 30-50 plus words would work best for you.

Always articulate in the first-person narrative. Remember, your story is more authentic when you tell it.

Quite recently, LinkedIn introduced another option, which allows you to upload multimedia stuff under the about section. You can upload rich media, such as photos, videos, website links, or presentations that help to make your story fancy and lively.

To add media samples simply click the plus icon on the top of "Featured" section. Click the pencil icon to edit existing files. You can add a link or link to external documents, photos, sites, videos, and presentations. Simply click on upload and browse files from your computer. You can also add a description of your upload.

vi. Work Experience

If you add or update your current work experience, it can lead to eight times more profile views and five times more messages that may create opportunity on LinkedIn.

Simply follow LinkedIn guidelines and steps while creating your profile to make it optimum. It is not rocket science, so keep it simple and agile. Mention your job title, employment type, company and location. Enter your start date and end date, if it is not your current job. Then incorporate your job description or key responsibilities. Always speak in the first-person narrative. Your outcomes, achievements, impression and experience are more reliable when they come from you. Write short paragraphs in a story format to give your career journey a life. Do not just copy-paste your job description. Focus on accomplishments and achievements. Describe key projects, deliverables and outcomes. Focus on your value addition in your current role.

A role can be easily added, modified or removed. In the case of multiple positions in the same entity, LinkedIn automatically combines or groups together. Jobs that are to be grouped should be identified within one month.

You will not be able to automatically represent changes to the English profile of your secondary language profile if you have built a profile in another language. If you change any place in the experience section of your profile, you will need to update your secondary language profile manually.

vii. Education Section

Pragmatic area to highlight your educational background. To enter your degrees and qualifications, simply follow the guidelines provided by LinkedIn or follow the steps while creating your profile.

After all, you invested time and money to attain specific qualifications, why not showcasing them the appropriate way. You can add, amend, or delete an education entry on your profile. Enter your School, College or University name and mention the name of qualification, for example, masters or bachelors degree. Don't forget to enter the start and end date in addition to your field of study and grades. LinkedIn also gives you the option to describe your extracurricular activities to showcase your additional talents. Sections related to description and media are instrumental in creating your story and precisely state your areas of specialisation, projects and subjects which you completed during your degree program. Make use of all the available sections to boost your profile.

viii. Licences & Certifications

In my opinion, it's one of the critical sections which can help you big time to build your personal brand over this platform. Certifications and Licences are valuable to create your competitive edge in the job search. You can demonstrate your niche, job-related certifications and licences, which may set you apart from other applicants.

When you complete a course or qualification with one of the LinkedIn partners, you will be contacted to add the accomplishment to your profile automatically.

To start the process, click the link in the email. LinkedIn can allow you to subscribe. Type the information requested. The details about qualification and degree will no longer auto-fill. However, you may manually enter the relevant information.

ix. Endorsements

It's useful to add capabilities on your profile. Adding skills to your profile enables you to highlight your abilities, strengths, and expertise, and to build your credibility in front of recruiters. Someone validating the skillsets helps to build trust in your professional experience and adding critical skills to enhance your profile visibility index. According to LinkedIn, members with five or more skills listed are 27 times more discoverable in searches on LinkedIn and receive up to seventeen times more profile views. Once you add a skill to your profile, that skill can be endorsed by your professional community.

Remember, only your first-degree connections can

recommend you for a skill. Skills endorsements strengthen your profile and increase the possibility that you'll be discovered for opportunities.

x.   Power of Recommendations

Trustworthiness is described as the quality of being entrusted and believed in. Recommendations are great to enhance the credibility of your profile and enhance the element of trust. It acknowledges the great work you've done. It's always great to have someone else's view about your strengths and accomplishments from their viewpoint. So think about people who could recommend your work and skills. Find out people in your professional circle like associates, supervisors, managers, leaders, partners. Those who have operated jointly with you and can talk about your abilities, intensities, results, and experience.

Job Searching on LinkedIn

LinkedIn helps you find and interact with the prospects to progress your career with over 3 million job postings. Learn about the keyword, title or location-based job quest.

LinkedIn will allow you to find positions that are important to your interests and qualifications. You can browse for jobs through the search field on the LinkedIn homepage or enter the jobs page directly, where you can check and apply for relevant positions. Millions of jobs are posted every day on LinkedIn. Moreover, it is crucial that you can find the right job postings to suit your needs and expectations.

To search for a job:

- o Click the Jobs icon at the top of your LinkedIn homepage.
- o Click the Search jobs field and enter keywords or a company name.
- o Enter the job location that you prefer in the Search location field and click Search.
- o Use the filters options at the top of the search results page to filter the results.
- o Click the job posting to view the job description and apply for the job if the job suits your requirement.

LinkedIn is dedicated to safeguarding users 'data. When looking and applying for LinkedIn positions, no changes are exchanged with your network. Check the existing anonymity and settings to know more.

Please notice that your transaction is private by design if you are beginning a job search on LinkedIn. When you apply for a position, no alerts will be provided to your network. You may also post an update from your LinkedIn profile if you want your network to realise that you are currently searching for a career.

Of the following purposes, you should test the existing privacy settings.

- o Share your profile edits
- o Select who can see your connections
- o Manage your recommendations
- o Select the types of messages you're willing to receive

You will either not show the community emblem on your profile or block alerts being received when you join a group while you are involved in groups of job seekers at LinkedIn.

Job Applications

Through using your LinkedIn profile, you can conveniently apply for vacancies. Find information about applying for jobs, sharing your resume and many more.

You can promptly apply for jobs on LinkedIn in case of the relevant position according to your desires. You will see an Easy Apply or Apply option depending on what the recruiter wants.

You cannot delete or change your application submitted through LinkedIn after applying. You have to contact the job poster directly through InMail.

Perform LinkedIn search to filter the relevant postings.

- o You may click on the job title to review the details and requirements.

- o In case you see Easy Apply button, it means that you can conveniently apply via your LinkedIn profile.

- o Otherwise, you will be routed to the company's website or third-party platform by clicking the apply button.

- o Follow the instructions and provide necessary the information.

- o Do not forget to review your job application before clicking the Submit Application button.

Job Alerts or Notifications

You can set LinkedIn job notifications that suit your expectations. You can set up alerts daily or weekly and choose to receive them via email, app notifications, or both.

You can create job alerts based on:

- o Job search
- o Automatic job alerts, if you have set your profile open for new job opportunities
- o You may also create job alerts for specific companies by visiting their career pages on LinkedIn

Contact Recruiters

Now, LinkedIn is adding a new function for members, where you can send a message to the recruiter directly if your skills match those listed job posting.

If your abilities and qualifications conform to those specified in the job posting. You may directly send the message to the recruiter. LinkedIn proposes to you that the job posting is a good fit and allows you to contact the job poster. These messages are free, and no InMail credits are needed. You can simply click and message job poster and avail of this opportunity.

Salary Insights

LinkedIn Salary gives you insights into the salary and the factors that contribute to making your career choices. Learn more about anonymity, access to salary information and the submission of your salary data.

LinkedIn asks members to provide their salary details to

create this data. When you enter your salary information. LinkedIn Salary gives you insights into compensation values for particular employment and various factors influencing the pay scale, such as location, years of experience, sector, business size and level of education. They also use this data to provide you with customised features and suggestions.

You can also add additional incentive details when submitting your salary details, such as sign-on rewards, company shares and more.

On LinkedIn Salary, you can find additional salary details and patterns. Which can help you gain a better understanding of how your salary compares with those in the similar profession.

Once you enter your salary information, you may view what members earn as average for a specific job. You will be able to view the following information:

- o **Basic or Base salary**
- o **Total compensation**
- o **Additional compensation such as bonus, commission etc.**

Moreover, depending on the type of information available, you can also see the following:

Company salaries: Dive into insight pages for companies to explore how salaries differ within companies.

Factors that may influence salary: Factors that may

affect the salary for a given title in a region include the size of a business, sector, level of education, and field of study, for example.

Top-paying jobs: Find out which locations pay higher for a job and see how many job openings are there.

Open jobs: You will also see current job openings for your role and desired location.

Data Security & Protection

Any salary details that you submit to LinkedIn is confidential and cannot be used by any other person. It will not be added to your LinkedIn profile.

Your payment information is encrypted. The salary information that you provide is combined with other participants 'data to measure their insights into factors like title, company, location and skills. These can also be used to provide extra features and instructions depending on your salary.

Recruiters will not be in a position to monitor or access your personal payment details. Actually, nobody can see your particular salary details. Any salary details you send to LinkedIn remains private. Salary data can only be interpreted as a part of aggregations by recruiters to compile summary.

Job Recommendations

LinkedIn's algorithm can support you in connecting with jobs that suit your profile and skillset. It also gives you the option to adjust your choices and preferences depending on the factors like your location, experience, and industry.

The Positions "You May Be Interested In" feature shows jobs that suit your profile published on LinkedIn. You will locate this feature in the LinkedIn feeds on the homepage by selecting Jobs at the top of your homepage. You may also subscribe for LinkedIn Premium to optimise job search and get access to many other features.

Chapter Five

JOB INTERVIEWS

We all know about the job interviews; they play an integral role in the hiring process. What is the history of job interviews? How, did they evolve?

At the beginning of humanity, it was all about the hunting of food instead of job hunting, because there were no jobs available. The only job available was to search for food to survive. In that era, life revolved around food, so men hunted while women gathered food. Nevertheless, it was not that simple as it sounds.

If we study the history of ancient Egypt, Greece and Rome, we realise that they required workers to carry on their work. From 1700 to 1800 BC, professions were passed on from generation to generation. When humans advanced and developed from Hunter-Gatherer stage to the era of cultural development and began to allocate professions to certain individuals, the passing on of these roles from generation to generation was the norm. In short, people were born into their job. If your father was the blacksmith, you learned to become the next blacksmith, and so on. It was tough to challenge the norms of society. To get out of the profession of your ancestors was just like a vicious circle. People were tagged and staged in a society based on their professions, which served as their identity. The whole process activated the transportation of conventional wisdom, trade and skills from one generation to the other. Job openings or vacancies were created, when tradesmen did not have children. They passed on their profession to apprentices. In reality, apprenticeships were less like internships and more of a binding contract of servitude.

That was just the beginning, since then the process has come a long way. Industrial revaluation, globalization, advancement in technology and innovations have not only changed the way, we live but also the way we communicate and interact. Process of job interviews also gone into the process of continuous improvement and evolved with technology.

Telephone and internet redefined the interview style and process. Face-to-face, traditional interviews were replaced with virtual and telephonic interviews to avoid travelling time and costs. Candidate's assessments tests were also redefined by introducing online screening tools. In 1995, internet and video technology evolved and the first public video conference between North America and Africa took place.

Later on, in 2003, LinkedIn completely changed the perspective of job hunting and job publishing and provided a platform for job seekers and employers to connect. YouTube, Facebook, Twitter, Skype and smartphones entirely transformed almost everything around us and created a visible impact on job hunting and interview tools and techniques.

Today, jobs are being published, promoted, through various social media platforms. Furthermore, candidates are being sourced and interviewed by using every bit of technology available in the market. Nevertheless, despite changing technology, the interview will continue to be a central part of the hiring process.

Power Pack Interview Mantra

It is great to have a spot on the interview table. This shows that you brand yourself in the right way, in the right direction and interact with the relevant people. You may just be fortunate, but undoubtedly, it means you do many good. It is now time to turn to an interview mode, and that will start just before you reach their doors, grab your cell phone or get on the video interview platform.

The interview stage is the most important and crucial in the job acquisition process. Regardless of technological advances, virtual platforms, and still face-to-face job interview is one of the most popularly used methods for the employees' selection. Never ever, go to an interview unprepared. Key to success is effective planning and rigorous preparation, before the interview. During my career in Human Resources, I have come across many candidates, who come for an interview with no knowledge about the company and its business, and many times not even sure, about the position they have applied for. Trust me, your lack of knowledge about the company and the position does not leave a positive impression on the recruiter. Usually, the recruiters do the screening by evaluating the candidates based on personality and general knowledge about the company and the industry and shortlist for the second interview with the hiring/line manager for the evaluation of technical and job-related skills and knowledge. In case you failed to impress the recruiter, you cannot get through to the second level.

Stage I

Pre Interview Phase

"By failing to prepare, you are preparing to fail."

Benjamin Franklin

No matter, you are a fresher or a seasoned professional; consider this phase more important than the interview. Your hard work and dedication during this stage guarantee your success in the interview stage. Firstly, plan your interview preparation methodology and technique. Secondly, execute your plan in a timely and systematic manner. You need to know a couple of things before getting yourself on the interview table, position that you are being interviewed for, and the company. Go through the job advertisement carefully and try to understand the requirements of the job in detail, not only the technical knowledge but also the required skills and competencies.

i.   Research

As you know that "Ignorance of Law is not an excuse", in this era of information, technology and digitalisation, not having information about the potential employer is not an acceptable excuse. Do a proper research and homework to know the business line and corporate culture of your potential employer. Get on the internet and go through the company website in detail, begin from the history of the organisation, management, products & services, solutions and geographical locations. Download the annual reports and review them carefully to know the financial situation of the company. All responsible and good companies publish their annual reports on the website to share it with customers, clients and shareholders. Believe me, this research and study are not useless, you are actually preparing yourself for one of the most common, frequently asked, in-fact, must interview question; "What do you know about our Company?" alternatively, "Do you know about the business of our Company?" If you are prepared well and up-to-date, this question will give you a chance to impress the interviewer, and if you do not prepare well, it can lead to a nightmare.

ii. Understand Job Requirements

Do not underestimate the job advertisement, because many questions revolve around the job specification and job description. Do thorough homework on the technical requirements of the job, required knowledge, skills and abilities and try to build your answers based on your qualification or relevant experience. Most of the interviews revolve around the evaluation of skills and personality. Some employers prefer relevant skills, while others focus on a vibrant personality. Because they strongly believe, that personality is crucial and skills can be developed through training, coaching and mentoring. Nevertheless, there is no harm in researching about the specific job and developing a comprehensive knowledge base related to the best practices in your profession. Again, you are preparing yourself for the most important question; "How can you contribute towards the success of our organisation?"

On the other hand, "Why should we hire you?"

Stage II

Interview Phase

"A job interview is a two-way communication to probe for cultural and team fit. No matter which side of the table you sit, you should be asking questions that are important to you without fear."

Salil S. Jha

Let us discuss the "Show Time"; it is your chance to turn around the things your way. You cannot get a job without an impressive interview. Moreover, the word "Interview" strikes terror into the heart of many - if not most - job hunters. You can overcome your worries by considering the interview more like a conversation, with employers and most particularly with the person who has the power to hire you. In the era of digitalisation and globalisation, interviews may be face-to-face or online. A huge percentage of employers also conduct interviews via digital platforms, Skype, Zoom and many others. So please do not hesitate to enhance your knowledge about these digital communication tools to avoid any confusion during the actual interview. Try mock interviews with your friends, colleagues or family members to get rid of anxiety.

Interview process and style vary from company to company, country to country. It may simple or complex depending on the size of the organisation. You should always ready for a series of interviews, panel interviews or cross-functional interviews.

Some basic principles are below, whether an interview is being conducted by the Executives or Hiring Manager.

o   Believe that any person you confront will contemplate everything from the host to the copier to the hiring manager. If you really want the work, all these members must be given a massive first impression. So, enter with positive body language, be respectful and welcoming.

o Next, focus on answering each question taking into account the critical deliverables of that job. Tell me about yourself; for example, when they say that, they are not looking for a walk line-by-line along with your resume. They want to know you as a person and professional highlight your strengths, achievements and significant projects in your previous roles. If you know that this job requires excellent communication and an ability to get along with all types of people, give references and quote examples from your professional journey. Try to correlate your existing or previous roles and focus on transferable skills.

o Try to introduce the element of fun and make the conversation pleasant and delightful. Interviewers are not there only to reject you; instead, they are taking time away from their busy schedules to check your eligibility for the role. If you make it warm, genuine, and a little fun-oriented, you will likely be able to create a lasting impression.

o No harm in asking again if you do not understand the question. You should always ask for clarification to answer the question correctly. No one is expecting you to be a computer.

o   Do not jump to the conclusion and expect a job offer right in the beginning after the success of just one interview. Remember, organisations perform series of interviews, so it is very important to maintain the positive energy and right attitude until the last interview.

Online Interview Skills

Digital transformation and social media enable employers to conduct frequent remote interviews. It has become a new normal during COVID-19 crisis. You will definitely come across audio or video interview before a face-to-face conversation. Typically, this is before you go in person, but sometimes even after that. Nailing these remote interviews is a skill you can learn with some practice, so I suggest you practice a mock interview with a friend. Ensure right IT infrastructure. Evaluate in advance, if your land or mobile line is in good working order, with a high signal wherever you go to the interview. Cafes or co-working spaces are not suitable for purpose if they do not have quiet areas and excellent internet connectivity. In the same way, test your computer, laptop or smartphone and do not forget the check the audio/video settings.

Be punctual and flexible, ensure to get ready at least ten to fifteen minutes before the interview to avoid any surprises. Be flexible to wait for ten to fifteen minutes or even more after the start time. Remember, interviewers are also human, and they may be having a busy schedule or technical issue. Focus more on the surroundings and background and lighting, especially during video calls. Select a quiet place to avoid noisy surroundings that can distract the interviewer and ensure that nothing wrong appears.

The trick to successfully completing these interviews is to behave polite, relaxed and approachable. Here are a couple of tips.

o   Do not forget to smile while you talk. If you are smiling during the conversation, you will sound like a pleasant conversationalist, not a nervous interviewee.

o   As I mentioned earlier, do not underestimate the power of light and gentle humour. Try to introduce a bit of fun in conversation.

o   Just be yourself and act trustworthy and practical. Interviewers do not feel comfortable with anxious and confused people. They like genuine individuals with whom they can enjoy a cup of coffee.

o   To develop a rapport during remote interviews is tough so prepare some powerful stories relating to your professional portfolio in advance. Remember, it is your turn to personally brand yourself and propagate your relevance for the role you are being interviewed for. Think how you want them to remember you after the conversation and try to leave a lasting and positive impression. In the end, do not forget to pay thanks to the interviewer for their time.

o   Post interview conversation is also very crucial and

helpful to ensure next level conversation. After a reasonable time, send a thank you note and demonstrate your willingness for further process, if you wish to do so.

Onsite Interview

Also referred to as "personal interview" this is the most common form of interview and is usually held face-to-face in the company's offices. Find out the estimated length of the meeting to be prepared; the duration varies from 30 to 90 minutes. Shorter interviews would mean giving concise responses. More extended interviews will provide you with more time to go into depth and help your answers with examples. In-person interviews usually happen at the employer's location, show up fifteen to thirty minutes before.

1. Dress to Impress

Research about the dressing norm in the company you are going for an interview. If you do not know, ask and inquire about the office outfit. It shows you are thinking forward and prevents you from showing up in a blazer in an office where the casual dressing is in trend. Take out the relaxed outfit that makes you look smart, practical and professional. Avoid wearing clothes, which do not go with the occasion. I have seen people turning up in clothes, which are not meant for an interview.

2. Positive Body Language

In the interviews, establish good eye contact, smile, and friendly handshake with any person you encounter. Imagine an interview like a discussion where you can highlight the key points that you want to present and also market yourself and get answers to your questions.

3. Communication Style

Research shows 50-50 rule is very practical and successful. It means half the time you listen carefully, half the time you talk in the interview. According to the report, people who did not take this combination were those who were not recruited. Balance is the key here; when you say too little, you find yourself trying to conceal something about your past. In addressing the interviewer's questions, follow the "twenty-second to two-minute rule." Studies have demonstrated that when it is your turn to talk or answer a question, you will intend not to talk longer than two minutes at a time if you wish to make the greatest impression. An outstanding answer to the interviewer's question often takes just twenty seconds. No less than that, because otherwise you will be perceived as a poor communicator.

4. Interviewer's Style

Quickly interpret and adjust to the personality of the interviewer. Some people prefer fast and concise responses and many others like stories and facts. Analyse whom you are talking to, what are their patterns of voice and preferred style? Your goal is to fit that theme and tone. An interviewer, who interrupts you to ask another question, or to redirect, needs your responses quicker and more specific. Success factor here is that you need to be very versatile and flexible to reinvent your way and fulfil interviewer's expectations.

"Everything on your résumé checks out to be factual and accurate. I'm afraid you're just not cut out for the advertising business."

COMMOM INTERVIEW QUESTIONS

The most important, first and foremost question, interviewers may ask you is, "Tell me about yourself." How you respond to this item will determine your destiny during the remainder of the interview. So, here are some tips you need to hold in mind about your responses to this critical question. In my view, every job interview conversation begins with this question, directly or indirectly. Wording may vary but the theme remains the same.

- ***Tell me about yourself.***

    This question is entirely open-ended and a kind of test for you. The interviewer wants to see how you react and answer to an unstructured scenario. Cross-question instead of a structured response is a definitely wrong way to answer this fundamental question. It clearly shows that you have no idea how to respond to an uncertain and unstructured situation.

    The ideal response to this question is to express your professional experience, skills, and knowledge. Therefore, the interviewer could correlate and match your answer with the job requirements. The interviewer is interested in your career summary, and more particularly, in your professional profile and its relevance with the position.

    Best way to prepare this answer lies in the job

requirements. Find out the required competencies and skills for the job and then embed them in your reply. Use this question to propagate your personal brand. Your focus should be to convince the interviewer in a strategic manner by highlighting the aspects of your profile that are relevant for the job. Prepare your answer in advance and keep it crisp and crystal, concise and fluent. It should come spontaneously and with ease to impress the interviewer. Focus on your strengths, transferable skills and summarise your professional career wisely. Remember, this question will set the tone.

Super Five (5)

There are multiple questions and variables, which interviewers may ask depending on their style or job requirements, and the list is enormous. Nevertheless, you can prepare these five fundamental and common questions. Most of the time, the whole interview revolves around these big five questions, I call them "Super Five".

1. *Why are you interested in our organisation?*

   Purpose of this question is to understand your motive to apply in a certain organisation. Why a position in this company, and why not in any other. It is a great chance for you to show the interviewer, how much you know about them, organisational values and culture.

How your personal values are aligned with their corporate values? Remember, employers like those who like them. Again, the ideal answer to this question demands research about the potential employer well before showing up in an interview.

2. **What value can you add to our business?**

Interviewers want to know what is in for them if they decide to hire you. What would be the return on if they give you this opportunity? Best chance to prove your eligibility for the role and convince them, how you could be a great resource for them. Give reference from your past projects and explain how part. Tell them, how you can assist them in current challenges and add value with your knowledge and skills.

3. **Tell us about your strengths and weaknesses.**

It is a personality-based question. The purpose is to evaluate, your personality traits and their alignment with the organisational culture. Do you have the right personality that makes other people coordinate with you easily? Are you a culturally fit candidate? Tell them about yourself and align your answer with the personality traits and competencies required for the role. If excellent communication is the key competency, they are looking in candidates, prove to them that you are a great communicator and knows the art of interaction and networking.

4. ***Why should we consider you on other candidates?***

What is your competitive edge? Obviously, you are not the only one applying for a certain role, there are many other applicants competing with you. Therefore, it is very important for the interviewers to identify that you are the best person. Explain them with examples and references and convince them, what differentiates you from others. Personality is one of the key deciding factors in the success of an interview. Tell the interviewer that you are the right person to carry out this role and having the right set of personality traits.

5. ***What are your expectations?***

Most of the companies define a certain budget for every position and it is very important for them to know the financial expectations of the candidates. Whether they afford you or your expectations are much higher than their defined budget.

TOP 5 INTERVIEW QUESTIONS...

YOU SHOULD ASK DURING THE INTERVIEW!

what is the job
description?

What are the core
competencies a
person should have
to perform this job?

Are these the sorts of
individuals I might
want to work with, or
not?

If everything goes fine,
would I be able to
influence them?

Would I be able to
persuade them to offer
me the compensation I
expect?

Interview Questions You Should Ask

More or less all job interviews are a two-way discussion; here you will find top five questions that you may ask to the interviewer.

1. *What is the job description?*

   You need to know precisely what assignments and tasks will be asked of you. What are the job requirements? Therefore, you can decide whether these are the activities you might genuinely want to do, and can do.

2. *What are the core competencies a person should have to perform this job?*

   You need to see whether your abilities coordinate those that the employer thinks a high performer in this position must have, to carry out this responsibility well.

3. *Are these the sorts of individuals I might want to work with, or not?*

   Do not overlook your instinct on the off chance that it discloses to you that you would not be open to working with these individuals! You need to know whether they have the sort of characters that would empower you to achieve your best work. On the off chance that these individuals are not it, continue looking!

4. *If everything goes fine, would I be able to influence them?*

I have a competitive edge that makes me unique as compared to other individuals?" You have to consider carefully, what makes you not quite the same as other individuals who can do a similar activity.

For instance, if you were great at dissecting issues, how would you do that?

(1) Carefully?

(2) Instinctively, instantly? Or on the other hand

(3) By counselling with more prominent experts in the field

You see the point. You are attempting to put your finger on the "style" or "way" in which you do your work. This signifies how you do it. That is particular and ideally engaging; with the goal that they pick you over other individuals, they are meeting.

Stage III

Post Interview Phase

*"Success is not final, failure is not fatal: it
is the courage to continue that counts."*

Sir Winston Churchill

The interviewer should be tracked, steadily and tactfully. For example, wait for a follow-up interview or decision without losing your temper or being frustrated or angry. It does not mean blackmailing the organisation, which would probably ruin your chances of success. The post-interview stage begins as soon as you exit the interview room. Write down things you feel you need to ask and take notes about everything.

Remember, various employers have very different ways to handle the post-interview phase. Some employers may send you official acknowledgement by email or post, while others may rely on the hiring manager to give you a personal note and still others do not have any formal procedure. Every answer (except everlasting silence) automatically indicates that an interview has succeeded or failed.

Thank You Note

If you want to stand out from other candidates, do not underestimate the power of thank-you notes. Trust me, interviewers like to receive respectful email from the candidates. As during the interview phase, you were trying to convince the interviewers regarding your excellent communication skills and working with people from diverse background etc. Thank-you note will prove your claim by creating a positive impression on the interviewers. It also shows that you know the value of their time and effort in order to evaluate for a certain role.

It also makes them recall you while filling-out the interview assessment forms and differentiate you from other candidates.

Interview notes are also very helpful to cover-up anything that you missed or to elaborate on something which is very important for them to know about you.

Finally yet importantly, employers are keen on intact talent relationship management. If you feel that you are suitable for the current role, but you definitely want to apply for a future and more relevant position. Then thank-you note is your go-area.

I Initiate — *Positively*

N Narrate — *Honestly*

T Tolerate — *Disagreements*

E Examples — *As Reference*

R Realistic — *Preview*

V Value — *Experience*

I Illustrate — *Strengths*

E Eagerness — *In Body Language*

W Windup — *Sensibly*

Behavioural Interview

Behavioural-based interviews are focused on figuring out how the interviewee behaved in different circumstances related to work. Such interview correlates past with future. It means that how you have acted in the past determines how you would act in the future.

Job seekers also wonder whether a typical job interview and a behavioural interview vary. How would you do to prepare for the behavioural questions from the employer?

Within the current style of the work interview, there is no difference. The difference is the kind of questions posed for the interview.

Behavioural interview questions allow applicants to share examples of different circumstances in which those skills had to be used. The response "can have a verifiable, tangible proof as to how an applicant has dealt with previous issues," says the Society for Human Resource Management. In short, it is a way to show what you can do for this potential employer in the future with your past job results.

It is always tricky to answer questions with proper reference and context. Besides, to build a connection with the requirements of the position, you are considering. The best way is to tackle the questions of the behavioural interview is "STAR Interview Method".

STAR Interview Method

The STAR interview method provides a simple way to address behavioural interviews, which asks you to demonstrate how you treated a particular situation in the past.

The concept of a suitable example is just the beginning of your discussion. Then you must share the information, without unnecessary rushing, in a convincing and easy-to-understand way. That is precisely what you can do with the STAR method. "It is useful because it offers a straightforward context to help an applicant relate a relevant tale of earlier job experience.

It is easier to share a concise reaction by using these four components to form your story and give the interviewer "a convincing and digestible description".

Situation: Paint the picture and quote a relevant example.

Task: Explain in this situation what your duty is.

Action: Clarify precisely what you have done to deal with it.

Result: Share the effects of your actions.

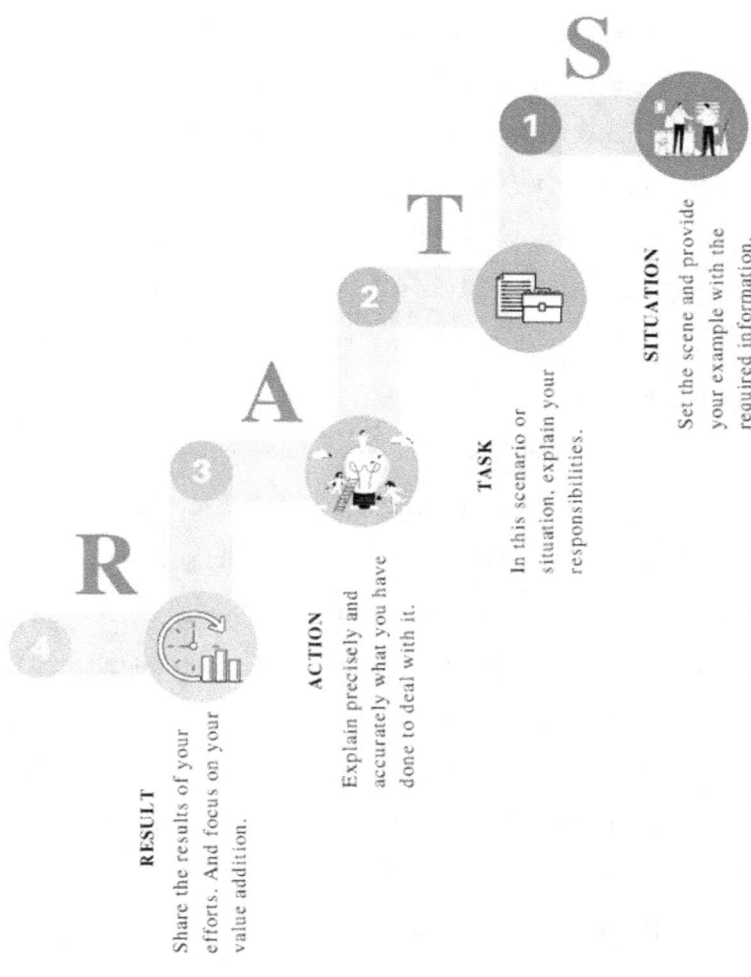

S

SITUATION

Set the scene and provide your example with the required information.

T

TASK

In this scenario or situation, explain your responsibilities.

A

ACTION

Explain precisely and accurately what you have done to deal with it.

R

RESULT

Share the results of your efforts. And focus on your value addition.

It is just the first step that you know what the acronym means; you must know how to use it. To provide the best answers by using this method, follow this systematic process.

1. Quote relevant example

If you use it to structure, the answer using a very non-relevant anecdote, then the STAR interview method is not helpful. That is why you must find a suitable scenario for your professional history.

You cannot know exactly what the respondent is going to ask you ahead of time. It is smart to have a variety of stories and explanations available for you to tweak and adapt to various questions.

2. Set the scene

It is time to set the scene with your anecdote selected. It is tempting, particularly if your nerves get the best from yourself, to add all kinds of unnecessary details.

Your aim is to paint a clear picture and highlight the complexities of the situation in which you are living, so it appears that the result you will touch is far more profound. Keep things concise and concentrate on what your story undeniably matters.

3. Explain your role

For a cause, you are telling this story, you were involved in it. That is what you mean when you let the interviewer know precisely where you are.

The "action" part of the response can easily be confused. This part, however, aims at describing your specific roles in this particular scenario and any goals that have been set for you before you get into what you actually did.

4. Highlight your actions

What steps have you taken to achieve this goal or to solve it? Resist the urge to give a straightforward or glossy-out response such as "I have worked hard on it, therefore ..." or "I have studied very ..." This is your chance to express some unique features. Dig deeply and make sure you give enough information on what you did exactly. Has a certain team worked with you? Did you use a particular software? You formulated a comprehensive strategy. That is what your interviewer would like to know.

5. Explain the benefit

Now it is time to be cheerful and explain how you have improved positively. The last part of your response should focus on the consequences of your actions.

Even when it comes to a time when you have failed or mistaken, be sure to finish up highly by discussing, what did you learn from this failure?

Please note interviewers do not just care what you did; they want to know also, why it was relevant. So make sure you take stock of the results and quantify them if you can. The statistics still have an effect.

> **"Tell me when you reached a goal that you felt was out of reach at the beginning."**

Situation

"My company has decided to concentrate on new customers and agreed to rapidly broaden its list of new customers in a highly saturated market."

Task

"As the sales director for my segment, my goal was to increase our new customers in just one quarter by at least 30%."

Action

"In coordination with my sales team and marketing department, I initiated a rigorous door to door campaign and also exploited the social media platforms. We also offered customers training at their site and enhanced the product portfolio to meet the needs of new customers."

Result

"Due to an effective marketing campaign and the introduction of new products, we raised the number of new customers quite significantly within three months. Our actual achievement was 10% higher than our targets."

COMMON BEHAVIOURAL INTERVIEW QUESTIONS

YOU MAY EXPECT DURING THE INTERVIEW!

Give an example when you've had to work together with someone whose temperament was really different from yours.

Describe a situation when you faced a disagreement while collaborating in a group. How did you cope with that?

Describe a time when you've been struggling to build a relationship with someone of importance.

Tell me about the time you needed somebody who wasn't responsive to information. What did you do?

COMMON BEHAVIOURAL INTERVIEW QUESTIONS
YOU MAY EXPECT DURING THE INTERVIEW!

Indicate a moment when making a positive impact on a customer was necessary. How have you done that?

Give me an example when you haven't fulfilled the demand of a client. How did you fix the problem?

Tell me how did you achieve customer satisfaction in your previous roles?

Describe a moment when a troublesome person needed to communicate. How did you treat it, and what was the situation?

COMMON BEHAVIOURAL
INTERVIEW QUESTIONS
YOU MAY EXPECT DURING THE INTERVIEW!

It is challenging to offer quality service while dealing with many customers. How do you balance the needs of your clients?

Tell me about a situation when you've been under enormous pressure. How did you get across it, and what was happening?

Describe a time that was transforming the team or organization. How have you been influenced, and how have you adapted?

Give me an example of a moment when you had to revisit your stance and get out of a tight or awkward situation delicately.

COMMON BEHAVIOURAL INTERVIEW QUESTIONS

YOU MAY EXPECT DURING THE INTERVIEW!

Tell me you've struggled for a while. How have you handled this?

Tell me about a time when you have had to be very careful to fulfil all the highest goals.

Describe the project you've run for a long time. How have you managed to keep everything running timely?

Give an example when you had too much to do in your basket. Sometimes everything on your to-do list is simply not possible.

COMMON BEHAVIOURAL INTERVIEW QUESTIONS

YOU MAY EXPECT DURING THE INTERVIEW!

Describe a time when you were a technical specialist. What did you do to ensure that everybody understood you?

Discuss a time when you had to focus on written correspondence to express your thoughts to your staff.

Give me an example of a time when a disappointed customer needed to describe something complicated. How did you deal with this sensitive situation?

Tell me a time when you were disappointed with your job. What did you do to boost your engagement?

Chapter Six

MONEY MATTERS

You have passed through the interview stage successfully and prove your expertise for the position, now it is time to review the job offer and salary. Always remember! Money matters always matter; career and financial growth go hand in hand. Salary negotiation stage is crucial because it can make or break your deal.

Before we discuss the salary negotiation techniques, it is important to understand how organisations define salary ranges, brackets or slabs. What are the different compensation strategies floating in the market?

What are the key differences in a fixed and variable salary, short term and long-term benefits?

Salary scales not only help organisations to control the staff cost but also assist to maintain pay equity among employees. Majority of the organisations design their compensation framework after careful market research, which reflects the company's belief and philosophy about compensation. How employers decide and determine what are they going to pay to their employees? What is the mentality and approach that control the compensation decisions? Some organisations design attractive combination of fixed and variable pay, while some try to attract talent by introducing above-average benefits schemes. It is the choice of the employer to be a paymaster, means paying more than the market rate or match the market standards with average pay scales. Some employers tend to be below the market average and attract the talent for so many other reasons. Paymasters tend to pay more than their competitors to attract and retain high calibre individuals or talent. Their hiring practices revolve around sourcing the talent, no matter, what it costs. They use above-average pay scales as an effective tool to win the War of Talent and target the trained employees working with competitors. Majority of the organisations strive to pay according to the market average, usually pay more or less similar, what their competitors are paying.

Many employers pay below-average salaries to confine their staff cost. Majority of the organisations do not even know, what is their position in the market in terms of salary and benefits unless they participate in the salary surveys.

Many organisations with a strong brand identity do not solely depend on pay scales to attract talent, but they also play based on strong brand name and organisational culture. Organisations decide their stance in the market, whether to lead or lag, and this becomes the pay strategy of the organisation.

HR Professionals mainly compensation & benefits specialists identify the pay rate and salary scales through various methods. Before you understand the salary negotiation tricks and techniques, it is important to understand the salary components and to know how organisations define the salary slots.

Compensation Package

Many companies focus on total rewards approach and offer a complete compensation package. Usually, they divide the salary into two major components, fixed and variable pay.

1. Fixed Pay

Fixed pay is paid to perform a specific job. Commonly known as base pay or basic salary, and does not change because of performance or achievement of objectives. It is decided mainly by the organisation's philosophy and pay structure according to the position or job. Basic salary varies from country to country.

2. Variable Pay

Many organisations pay a variable portion of compensation in the form of bonuses, incentives, sales commission, and profit-sharing plans etc. Terminology and methodology change according to the industry. For example, manufacturing companies usually pay bonus, while sales-oriented companies prefer to pay a sales commission to their sales staff.

Whether you call it profit sharing, bonus or sales commission, it generally depends on the performance. Sales commission is usually paid as a predefined percentage of achieved sales; a bonus is paid in a certain number of basic salaries. Profit-sharing is a form of variable pay provided to all employees based on the profits of the company.

Companies usually have predetermined goals and formulas for determining the amount that will be allocated to employees. Profit-sharing is typically implemented to achieve employee participation and engagement with the organisation's success.

Most of the companies set quarterly or yearly objectives or key performance indicators and calculate the variable compensation based on individual achievement against the predefined targets.

According to the research, variable pay is on the rise. The prevalence and variety of variable pay have increased over time, and data shows that variable pay continues to be a prominent player in the modern compensation landscape.

Approximately 74% of all organisations surveyed said that they offer some type of variable pay.

That number is even higher among top-performing companies — who are more likely to incorporate variable pay in their compensation strategies (82% versus 73% of typical companies). (Source: payscale.com)

3. Benefits

In addition to the fixed and variable compensation, successful companies also focus on comprehensive benefits schemes in the form of health insurance, wellness programs, and retirement benefits. We have many examples available in the market when companies try to get an upper hand in the war of talent by attracting and retaining talented individuals by offering above-average benefits. Some employers go beyond pensions, healthcare or company cars to attract new talent, according to a report.

More than a third of employees admit rewards and benefits are amongst their top consideration before accepting a new job, according to a survey of more than 1,000 people by Glassdoor, a recruiting website.

Many companies also provide standard benefits like housing allowance, mobile allowance, transportation allowance, mobile allowance, meal allowance etc. they usually depend on the requirements of the job and vary from company to company.

4. Work Life Balance

These days, work-life balance can seem like an impossible feat. Primary focus of work-life balance programs is to create a balance between personal and professional life.

It describes a variety of programs to help employees effectively manage personal and professional responsibilities without extreme stress or negative impact. Many organisations report that balancing work and family has overtaken other benefit and compensation items as a key factor in employee satisfaction and engagement surveys. Physical and emotional health has a direct linkage with employee engagement and performance.

Childcare facilities, flexible working hours and financial support programs are the examples of work-life balance initiatives. Significance and demand for work-life balance initiatives are increasing day by day. Good companies are taking meaningful approaches to enhance the spectrum of work-life balance. NIKE employee benefits vary by position, experience and location. However, some workers receive benefits like paid sabbaticals, fitness discounts and tuition assistance. All teams at Cisco are provided with a "Fun Fund" which can be spent on celebrations and fun activities.

American Express offers flexible work arrangements to some employees so that they can work on their own schedule. The Starbucks College Achievement Plan gives employees who work more than 20 hours a week the opportunity to complete a bachelor's degree with full tuition coverage for every year of college.

How Companies Design Pay Structure?

Organisations define and design their compensation framework and salary structure with the help of careful job analysis and benchmarking it with the market through salary surveys.

i.   Job Analysis

A job analysis is a process for gathering, documenting and analysing information to describe the jobs performed at an organisation. The basis of a job analysis is a job description. A job description describes the essential functions of a job as well as the frequency and importance of all tasks and responsibilities associated with a particular job.

ii.   Job Evaluation

A job evaluation is a systematic way of determining the value/worth of a job with other jobs in an organisation. It tries to make a systematic comparison between jobs to assess their relative worth for establishing a rational pay structure. This practice is quite common in many companies.

iii. Salary Surveys

Job evaluation, which is considered to determine the relative worth of a job within an organisation focuses on internal equity of compensation. While, remuneration surveys, commonly known, as salary surveys are useful to analyse the salary competitiveness with the external market. Remuneration surveys collect information on prevailing market compensation and benefits practices, including base pay, other cash payments, variable compensation (e.g., short and long-term incentive plans), and time off. Remuneration surveys allow organisations to recognise and relate their remuneration structures to local trends.

"If you hire me this week, I'm on special for only $3.99 a pound!"

Salary Negotiation

It is ideal to talk about salary at the end of the interview process, but it is tough to define the ending phase. In my opinion, do not initiate the salary discussion during the first interview. At the same time, neither you nor the employer is sure about the final decision. Best is to launch this discussion at the end of a whole series of interview.

When you are sure that the employer is going to propose an offer, whether it is after the first, the second or third interview. Then, is it time to answer the question that any employer eventually has to tackle: how much does that person cost me? Furthermore, you have the question: how much are they ready to pay me?

The employer may initiate a salary discussion by asking you this question:

- **How much are you expecting in terms of salary?**

  You may answer this question very tactfully, by saying that, it is premature to discuss salary until you decide to hire me. On the other hand, I choose to join your organisation.

  However, if the employer insists on having an answer to this question before proceeding further, then go for it. Let them know your expectations, but avoid giving a straight figure, instead mention a salary bracket or range. Tell them, I am looking for a salary ranging from this much to that much.

Sometimes, the employer already defines a salary bracket based on internal equity and willing to hire you immediately if you qualify and comes within their budget. However, in some instances, especially if the role is new and they do not have any internal reference to define the budget. Alternatively, they have not established any salary bracket then it is a different scenario and can lead to entirely open-ended discussions.

Remember that you should discuss salary only when you feel that you are the best available person to grab this job. You understand all the requirements, tasks and deliverables and finally yet importantly, you are willing to join them.

Don't Reveal Your Trump Card

Avoid mentioning your salary expectation first. As mentioned in many salary negotiation techniques, whoever mentions a figure first, lose the game. Your target should be that employer mentions the salary figure first.

In recent years, it has been found that where the targets are in the opposite direction, whoever first discloses the number, typically loses, you try to get the employer to pay as much as possible, and the employer wants to pay the least they can. A dozen hypotheses are already available about this topic.

Besides, many believe that it is true.

In the worst-case scenario, if you do not get a chance to play your game and you are bound to quote a figure, the ideal response is counter-question. You may ask them about the defined budget of this position.

Research Before You Negotiate

"Opportunity does not waste time with those who are unprepared." Never go unprepared, and without your complete toolkit. Always research about the company, market, salary brackets and salary ranges for certain roles. You can do it in many different ways, ask people who are already performing similar roles or perform an online search.

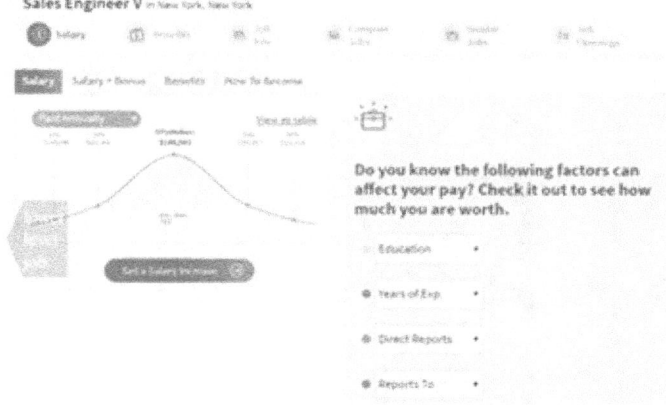

Remember, you will be on top of the salary discussion if you have already collected the necessary data. I personally do that, before accepting any role or while evaluating any job offer. Firstly, I check what the minimum or maximum salary for the position is. How much other companies of similar size and business are paying? As I mentioned earlier that you can employ the internet to assist you in your research. Trust me; there are multiple platforms available to extract this information based on roles etc.

www.salary.com my favourite platform. It is equally helpful for employers and job seekers. You can simply type in the role and location to get an overview of salary details.

www.payscale.com this is also very useful and user-friendly website to perform an internet-based search about salary scales.

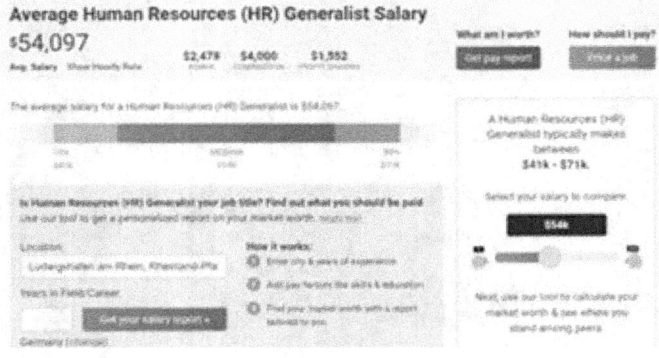

As I mentioned earlier, there are many platforms available, which allow you to perform extensive research based on many factors like location, industry, function and role.

You can also simply visit www.google.com and type in "Payscale in Germany", "Salary Range for HR Managers" or similar phrases, and it will automatically lead you towards the right platform.

Offline Research

You may get a lot more up-to-date information from people who do a similar job, maybe in another organisation or industry.

If you do not know where to find them, speak to people your connections, who might know someone. Professors and instructors typically know what their students do; you may also contact the career advisory in your College or University.

LinkedIn is also a useful platform in this regard. Approach your first-degree connections respectfully and request them to provide you with information, which you need to prepare yourself.

SALARY NEGOTIATION TIPS

Tip # 1

Do not underestimate the importance of friendliness. This sounds simple, but it is crucial: people are only going to fight for you because they like you. Anything you do in a negotiation that makes you less likeable increases the likelihood that the other side can try to get you a better deal. It is more than being polite; it is about managing some inevitable negotiating tensions. Such as asking for what you deserve without appearing greedy, pointing out gaps in the offer without looking petty, and being persistent without being a nuisance. Negotiators may usually prevent these traps by determining how others are likely to interpret them.

Tip # 2

It is crucial to know the current rate of pay for your position in your specific industry and in your geographic area. If you go through a pay negotiation without a figure, you are at the mercy of an experienced hiring manager who can literally manipulate the conversation. You may do so by looking online on sites such as Payscale or Glassdoor, or by asking someone in your profession.

Tip # 3

Enable them to understand precisely what you are asking makes sense. For employers to like you, it is not enough. You must also assume that the deal you want is worth it. Let your proposal always say the story that goes with it, just for yourself. Do not just state your preference, elaborate why it is justified. Explain why you deserve more money than other people you might have hired. It can be imprudent to make a request if you have no excuse.

Tip # 4

Show your keenness and interest and give them a clear signal that you are interested in the opportunity. People will not invest in a good or better deal if they think you would say "no thanks" at the end of the day. If you are seeking a better deal, make it clear that this employer is serious about you.

Tip # 5

Comprise the individual on the table. In addition, you have to understand him before you can influence the person who sits opposite you. What are the real goals and concerns? The interactions with a prospective manager vary considerably from those with an HR Director. You may encourage the latter to ask questions about the offer. Still, you do not want to annoy someone who might become your boss.

Tip # 6

Try to understand their limitations as well. They probably like you and may believe that you may deserve according to your expectations. They might have some salary caps or other reasons for not paying you desired package. Your job is to figure out when and where they are not flexible. When you speak to a big corporation that hires 10 similar people concurrently, you certainly will not get a higher salary than anyone else will. Nevertheless, other smaller companies may offer you some flexibility.

Tip # 7

Prepare yourself for the tough questions in advance. Do you have any other job offers? If we make an offer to you tomorrow, will you say yes? Are we the top choice? If you are rusty, you might say something inelegantly evasive or, worse, untrue. Never lie in salary negotiations. It always comes around to hurt you, but even if it does not, it is unethical and unprofessional. The other danger is that faced with a complicated issue, you may try too hard to satisfy yourself and end up losing advantage. You need to prepare yourself for the questions and problems that would place you on the defensive side, make you feel insecure or reveal your vulnerabilities.

Tip # 8

In case if an interviewer comes to you from an angle you did not anticipate, remember this basic rule: questioner's purpose and intent matters more than the question. The problem is always tricky, but the intent of the questioner is sincere. An employer who asks if you can accept the job offer instantly can simply be interested in knowing if you are very excited about the position. He is not trying to push you into a corner. A question as to whether you have other opportunities could be intended, simply to discover what sort of work you are looking for and if this business has a chance of attracting you.

Tip # 9

Unfortunately, "negotiating a job offer" and "negotiating a package" is synonymous to many people. Yet much of your work satisfaction comes from other variables that you can negotiate, perhaps even more quickly than your salary. Do not get fixed on your money. Focus on the value of the whole deal roles, place, transportation, flexibility in working hours, incentives for development and promotion, rewards, funding for continuing education, and so on. Always focus on the complete compensation package.

Tip # 10

I always say, when you try to get everything, you get nothing. Be wise in negotiation. When something is important to you, you must negotiate. However, do not haggle over every little thing. Fighting to get just a little more may harm people in the wrong way, and it can hinder your ability to bargain with an organisation later in your career. When it might matter more.

Tip # 11

One of the best ways to open discussions after you have received a job offer is to ask a meeting to discuss the proposal. Counter-offer discussion can be used to initiate a conversation to turn around things.

Tip # 12

If you are officially offered a position, do not rush to accept it immediately, if possible. Take advantage of this opportunity to ask follow-up questions, no matter how insignificant they might appear. Feel free to ask for more time to consider the bid, which means that you are careful and calculated in your dealings. The best way to obtain and use the extra time you need to make your decision is to confirm the employer's answer time. Ask for more details on the pay plan and workplace benefits, and enter into discussions on the offer and start date for your new work.

Tip # 13

It is natural to feel excited and anxious, but do not be so enthusiastic that you seem desperate. You do not know how many other applicants the hiring manager is interviewing, so play it cool. As I always say, the hiring managers may manipulate your desperation in many different ways. There is a fair chance that they will try to pay you less than your expectations and worth.

Tip # 14

Always speak the truth, no matter it hurts. I know, some people advocate other techniques and recommend exaggerating or over communicating. However, in my opinion, one should refrain from false claims. There are many simple ways to find out how much you are actually drawing, whether it is via a simple reference call or asking for a copy of your payslip. You do not want to lie about this issue. You do not want to start a new job with a lie on your record, either. Whether you are looking for a lower or higher position on the ladder, keep your arrogance in check, be prepared well advance, and be truthful about what you really want.

Tip # 15

Learn to say "no". You will reach a "walk-away point" If the final offer does not match your expectations. This may be dependent on financial necessity or market demand. Alternatively, simply what you need to feel good about your pay. It is never going to be easy to walk away from the bid, but it is essential to know when to do it, and powerful to be able to say "no."

References

10 Ways to Boost Your LinkedIn Profile To Get Hired!. Medium. (2020). Retrieved 28 April 2020, from https://medium.com/digital-vault/10-ways-to-boost-your-linkedin-profile-to-get-hired-358156db5d8c.

17 steps to a better LinkedIn profile in 2017. Business.linkedin.com. (2020). Retrieved 28 April 2020, from https://business.linkedin.com/en-uk/marketing-solutions/blog/posts/content-marketing/2017/17-steps-to-a-better-LinkedIn-profile-in-2017.

Arruda, W. (2020). *10 Outstanding Ways To Stand Out In A Job Search*. Forbes. Retrieved 28 April 2020, from https://www.forbes.com/sites/williamarruda/2015/11/11/10-outstanding-ways-to-stand-out-in-a-job-search/.

Associates, C. (2020). *Salary Range Structure Practices*. SHRM. Retrieved 28 April 2020, from https://www.shrm.org/ResourcesAndTools/hr-topics/compensation/Pages/SalaryRange.aspx.

Beatty, R. (2006). *The ultimate job search*. JIST Works.

BOLLES, R. (2018). *What color is your parachute? 2019: a practical manual for job-hunters and career-changers*. TEN SPEED Press.

Building a LinkedIn profile. Lynda.com - from LinkedIn. (2020). Retrieved 28 April 2020, from https://www.lynda.com/Business-Skills-tutorials/Building-LinkedIn-profile/693070/743794-4.html.

Building a LinkedIn profile. Lynda.com - from LinkedIn. (2020). Retrieved 28 April 2020, from https://www.lynda.com/Business-Skills-tutorials/Building-LinkedIn-profile/693070/743794-4.html.

Careers and Career Information - CareerOneStop. Careeronestop.org. (2020). Retrieved 28 April 2020, from https://www.careeronestop.org/.

Charlier, M. (2017). *Strengthen your LinkedIn profile*. Primento Digital.

Curriculum Vitae (CV) Format Guide: Examples and Tips | Indeed.com. Indeed.com. (2020). Retrieved 28 April 2020, from https://www.indeed.com/career-advice/resumes-cover-letters/cv-format-guide.

Dalton, S. (2020). *2-Hour Job Search, Second Edition : Using Technology to Get the Right Job Faster*. Ten Speed Press.

Dikel, M., & Roehm, F. (2004). *Guide to Internet job searching*. VGM Career Books.

Expected skills needs for the future of work. Deloitte Belgium. (2020). Retrieved 25 May 2020, from https://www2.deloitte.com/be/en/pages/public-sector/articles/upskilling-the-workforce-in-european-union-for-the-future-of-work.html.

Experience or education: which is more important?. Monster Career Advice. (2020). Retrieved 28 April 2020, from https://www.monster.co.uk/career-advice/article/experience-or-education-which-is-more-important.

Farr, J. (1995). *The quick interview and salary negotiation book*. JIST.

Future skills: Keeping the workforce human. Deloitte United Kingdom. (2020). Retrieved 25 May 2020, from

https://www2.deloitte.com/uk/en/pages/consulting/ar
ticles/future-skills-keeping-the-workforce-human.html.

Hess, A. (2020). *The 20 best companies for work-life balance.* CNBC.
Retrieved 28 April 2020, from
https://www.cnbc.com/2017/05/03/the-20-best-
companies-for-work-life-balance.html.

History of Job and Job Interview: Who Invented the Process?.
http://thespiritedhub.com/history-of-job-and-job-
interview-who-invented-the-process/

How to Establish Salary Ranges. Shrm.org. (2020). Retrieved 28
April 2020, from
https://www.shrm.org/mlp/pages/how-to-establish-
salary-ranges.aspx.

How to Establish Salary Ranges. Shrm.org. (2020). Retrieved 28
April 2020, from
https://www.shrm.org/mlp/pages/how-to-establish-
salary-ranges.aspx.

How to improve your CV layout | CVcorrect professional blog.
CVcorrect Blog. (2020). Retrieved 28 April 2020, from
https://www.cvcorrect.com/blog/4-top-tips-to-
improve-your-cv-layout/.

How to include certifications on a Resume | ResumeCoach.
https://www.resumecoach.com/write-a-
resume/certifications/

Hund, H. (2018). *Art of the job search.* [Heather Hund].

Job Hunting On Linkedin. Carehealthjobs.com. (2020). Retrieved
28 April 2020, from https://carehealthjobs.com/job-
hunting-on-linkedin/.

Job interview. En.wikipedia.org. (2020). Retrieved 28 April 2020, from https://en.wikipedia.org/wiki/Job_interview.

Kelley, T. (2017). *Get That Job : The Quick and Complete Guide to a Winning Interview.* Plovercrest Press.

Learn the Skills Your Industry Will Need in the Future. Harvard Business Review. (2020). Retrieved 25 May 2020, from https://hbr.org/tip/2018/06/learn-the-skills-your-industry-will-need-in-the-future.

Lee, D. (2020). *6 Tips For Better Work-Life Balance.* Forbes. Retrieved 28 April 2020, from https://www.forbes.com/sites/deborahlee/2014/10/20/6-tips-for-better-work-life-balance/.

Lewis, N. (2020). *Your CV - Education and Work Experience - career-advice.jobs.ac.uk.* career-advice.jobs.ac.uk. Retrieved 28 April 2020, from https://career-advice.jobs.ac.uk/cv-and-cover-letter-advice/your-cv-education-and-work-experience/.

Lewis, N. (2020). *Your CV - Education and Work Experience - career-advice.jobs.ac.uk.* career-advice.jobs.ac.uk. Retrieved 28 April 2020, from https://career-advice.jobs.ac.uk/cv-and-cover-letter-advice/your-cv-education-and-work-experience/.

Listing Professional Experience on Your Resume | Indeed.com. Indeed.com. (2020). Retrieved 28 April 2020, from https://www.indeed.com/career-advice/resumes-cover-letters/listing-professional-experience-on-your-resume.

Making your job hunting plan. Lynda.com - from LinkedIn. (2020). Retrieved 28 April 2020, from https://www.lynda.com/Business-Skills-tutorials/Making-your-job-hunting-plan/693070/743793-4.html.

Marr, B. (2020). *The 10 Vital Skills You Will Need For The Future Of Work*. Forbes. Retrieved 25 May 2020, from https://www.forbes.com/sites/bernardmarr/2019/04/2 9/the-10-vital-skills-you-will-need-for-the-future-of-work/#6f5745323f5b.

Marr, B. (2020). *The 5 Most Important Job Skills For The Future*. Forbes. Retrieved 25 May 2020, from https://www.forbes.com/sites/bernardmarr/2019/11/0 4/the-5-most-important-job-skills-for-the-future/#2b774d5f1e5d.

Martins, O. (2020). *History of Job and Job Interview: Who Invented the Process?*. The Spirited Hub. Retrieved 28 April 2020, from http://thespiritedhub.com/history-of-job-and-job-interview-who-invented-the-process/.

Martins, O. (2020). *History of Job and Job Interview: Who Invented the Process?*. The Spirited Hub. Retrieved 28 April 2020, from http://thespiritedhub.com/history-of-job-and-job-interview-who-invented-the-process/.

Resume Objective VS Summary Statement | ResumeCoach. ResumeCoach. (2020). Retrieved 28 April 2020, from https://www.resumecoach.com/resume-objective-vs-summary-statement/.

Resume Objectives: 70+ Examples and Tips | Indeed.com. Indeed.com. (2020). Retrieved 28 April 2020, from https://www.indeed.com/career-advice/resumes-cover-letters/resume-objective-examples.

Resume Profile vs. Objective (With Examples) | Indeed.com. Indeed.com. (2020). Retrieved 28 April 2020, from https://www.indeed.com/career-advice/resumes-cover-letters/resume-profile-vs.-objective-with-examples.

Resume Writing: Objectives, Summaries or Professional Profiles. GCFLearnFree.org. (2020). Retrieved 28 April 2020, from http://oer2go.org/mods/en-GCF2015/content/collections/resumewriting/2894/print.html.

Rock Your LinkedIn Profile - Who are you? Creating your profile summary. LinkedIn. (2020). Retrieved 28 April 2020, from https://www.linkedin.com/learning/rock-your-linkedin-profile/who-are-you-creating-your-profile-summary?autoplay=true.

The 10 skills you need to thrive in the Fourth Industrial Revolution. World Economic Forum. (2020). Retrieved 25 May 2020, from https://www.weforum.org/agenda/2016/01/the-10-skills-you-need-to-thrive-in-the-fourth-industrial-revolution/.

The 7 forces that will change the way you work. World Economic Forum. (2020). Retrieved 25 May 2020, from https://www.weforum.org/agenda/2018/09/here-are-seven-ways-your-job-will-change-in-the-future/.

The Curriculum Vitae: What are the most important aspects of your CV?. The Irish Times. (2020). Retrieved 28 April 2020, from https://www.irishtimes.com/student-hub/the-curriculum-vitae-what-are-the-most-important-aspects-of-your-cv-1.2483223.

The Top 10 Employee Perks and Benefits. Forbes. (2020). Retrieved 28 April 2020, from https://www.forbes.com/pictures/gkig45fhe/the-top-10-employee-perk/.

These are the best 20 best perks and benefits offered by top UK companies. The Independent. (2020). Retrieved 28 April 2020, from https://www.independent.co.uk/news/business/news/

google-asos-airbnb-20-best-perks-benefits-uk-employers-a6938716.html.

Thomas Edison conducted the first job interview in 1921 — here's how they've evolved since. Business Insider. (2020). Retrieved 28 April 2020, from https://www.businessinsider.com/evolution-of-the-job-interview-2015-5.

Variable Pay Is on the Rise: What the Data Show. PayScale. (2020). Retrieved 28 April 2020, from https://www.payscale.com/compensation-today/2017/09/variable-pay-rise-data-show.

What are the basic elements of a CV?. Monster Career Advice. (2020). Retrieved 28 April 2020, from https://www.monster.lu/en/career-advice/article/what-are-the-basic-elements-of-a-cv.

What is a resume? The essentials you need to know - SEEK Career Advice. Seek Career Advice AU. (2020). Retrieved 28 April 2020, from https://www.seek.com.au/career-advice/article/what-is-a-resume.

Work In Human Resources | The Best Job Hunting Site!. The Best Job Hunting Site!. (2020). Retrieved 28 April 2020, from https://bestjobhunting.com/work-in-human-resources/.

Writing a resume. Lynda.com - from LinkedIn. (2020). Retrieved 28 April 2020, from https://www.lynda.com/Business-Skills-tutorials/Writing-resume/693070/743795-4.html.

Subject Index

The Top 10 Best Websites for Jobs of 2020

- **Indeed**: Best Overall
- **Monster**: Runner-Up, Best Overall
- **Glassdoor**: Best for Employer Insights
- **FlexJobs**: Best for Remote Jobs
- **The Ladders**: Best for Experienced Managers
- **AngelList**: Best for Startup Jobs
- **LinkedIn**: Best for Connecting Directly With Recruiters
- **LinkUp**: Best for Up-to-Date Listings
- **Scouted**: Best for Recent College Graduates
- **Snagajob**: Best for Hourly Jobs